IDYLL BANTER

WEEKLY EXCURSIONS TO A VERY SMALL TOWN

CHRIS BOHJALIAN

IDYLL BANTER

WEEKLY EXCURSIONS TO A VERY SMALL TOWN

Harmony Books
NEW YORK

The columns in this book all appeared in the *Burlington Free Press* between 1989 and 2003, with the exception of the following longer essays, which appeared in the *Boston Globe* between 1993 and 2002: "Now That the Cows Are Gone"; "Losing the Library"; "Why the Green Mountains Turn Red"; "Of Memory and Hope"; "Untethered in Spain, Set Free on Route 66"; "Talking Then, Talking Now"; and "The Ladies' Room Just Inside Tomorrowland." In addition, "A Person Can Learn a Lot from Ian Freeman" is being published for the first time.

Text illustrations are details of *Stone City, Iowa* by Grant Wood; Joslyn Art Museum, Omaha, Nebraska.

Published by Harmony Books, New York, New York. Member of the Crown Publishing Group, a division of Random House, Inc.
www.crownpublishing.com

HARMONY BOOKS is a registered trademark and the Harmony Books colophon is a trademark of Random House, Inc.

Printed in the United States of America

Design by Lynne Amft

Library of Congress Cataloging-in-Publication Data
Bohjalian, Christopher A.
Idyll banter: weekly excursions to a very small town /
Chris Bohjalian. — 1st ed.
I. Title.
PS3552.O495I39   2003
813'.54—dc22   2003014941

ISBN 1-4000-5215-7

10 9 8 7 6 5 4 3 2 1

First Edition

For my friends—now family—here in Lincoln

If you don't know where you are,
you don't know who you are.

—WENDELL BERRY

Contents

Contents

THE SCHOOL—PLAYGROUNDS AND CLASSROOMS

THE LOCAL WILDLIFE

Contents

THE GREEN—AND THEN SPECTACULARLY YELLOW AND RED—MOUNTAINS

THE CHURCH WITH A WEATHERVANE ATOP THE STEEPLE

Contents

Contents

Foreword

YOUNG WRITERS ASK me frequently if I keep a writing notebook. Invariably I disappoint them when I tell them I don't. In
my library in my home there are no journals with snippets of dia-
logue I have overheard or sketches of characters I might someday
create. Occasionally I save the small (and long) sections that I
have chosen to delete from a novel I'm writing, but once the
book is complete I tend to recycle even those papers. (Yes, I
know: The archivist at the college where my papers are preserved
is going to call me the moment she reads this, and explain to me
in no uncertain terms what an egregious and irresponsible mistake I am making. She may be right. But I can't help but shud-
der when I envision some poor soul wasting months or years of
his life in a windowless room in the bowels of a brick monolith
examining the passages from my books that I chose to expunge.)

And I have never kept a personal diary.

Last year when I explained this to a reader in Vermont, she
corrected me. "Your weekly newspaper column is your diary," she
said. "That's your diary and your writing journal."

I had to ponder this for about a nanosecond before I realized
she was absolutely right. My Sunday column, "Idyll Banter," has
indeed been both a chronicle of my personal life and a compen-
dium of set pieces that have shadowed—foreshadowed, actually—
scenes and themes from my novels.

I have been writing "Idyll Banter" for the *Burlington Free Press*
since February 1992, and the column has appeared in the news-

1

paper's living section every single Sunday but two: once when we used the entire section for a lengthy year-in-review, and once when we profiled the steamboat *Ticonderoga* and needed every square inch of the section's front page for a diagram of the nineteenth-century paddlewheel steamer.

My original charge was, in the words of a paper's editor back then, "to write something that would make people who've lived their whole lives in Vermont smile. And people who've just come to the state. And, I guess, people who are visiting from out of town."

It's instructions that precise that make a columnist smile. I had a latitude that was agreeably broad, and twenty-one column inches—or roughly 675 words—a week.

I had lived in Vermont not quite six years at the time, a stretch that felt impressively lengthy to me then: It was, after all, about as long as I had lived anywhere else. I had two books behind me (including the single worst first novel ever published, bar none, an ill-conceived mystery about recent college graduates with the appalling pun for a title, *A Killing in the Real World*), and a third scheduled for publication that spring. With the hindsight of a person who has lived in one place now for close to two decades, I understand how swiftly six years pass and how little a person can know about a place in that time.

And place has always mattered greatly in my work, both in my fiction and my nonfiction. Certainly it has influenced these columns, in large measure because they are so keenly autobiographic. As Wendell Berry said, "If you don't know where you are, you don't know who you are."

I grew up in iconically Cheeveresque suburbs around New York City, while my wife spent her childhood in Manhattan itself. We arrived in Vermont as proudly downwardly mobile New Yorkers, essentially swapping a co-op in Brooklyn for a century-old Victorian with a slate roof and fish-scale trim in the middle of a Vermont village called Lincoln.

Lincoln is a special place. I hope it is not a unique one, however, if only because barely a thousand people live here and with the population of the earth fast approaching six billion, I would hate to think so few of us will ever have the chance to savor the sort of community I experience daily. We are a place in which the ladies' auxiliary of the volunteer fire company still holds a bake sale with cream cheese brownies at the polling station each election day, and we vote there with number-two pencils on paper ballots twice the size of diner place mats. We have a preschool that teaches the kids to sing "I Am a Pizza" in French and brings in a justice of the peace to marry the children's stuffed animals. At the general store, neighbors actually gather to discuss an ailing Latino cockatiel, and the store's owners know exactly where to find someone in a heartbeat who can milk a nursing llama mama with a baby more interested in pumpkin pine than llama manna. And every year on the Tuesday after Memorial Day, our elementary school—all 106 kids and the 14 teachers and administrators—walk en masse to the local cemetery to remember family and friends and, perhaps, find a few rusted G.A.R. stars beside the tombstones of the town's Civil War veterans.

My sense is that Lincoln shares certain universalities with small towns in (for example) Nebraska, New Mexico, and parts of New York: a powerful feeling of kinship; a tolerance for human eccentricity that is often unappreciated; and a glorification of neighborliness for the simple reason that it is easier to be civil than ornery when on any given day you're likely to run into someone at the library, the post office, or while watching the annual outhouse races—faux outhouses on wheels, a single person inside—that precede the local parade on the Fourth of July.

Besides, we need each other.

In the years since my wife and I first arrived in Vermont, there have been enormous changes on our planet, as well as here in the small world of Lincoln—and, of course, in the even tinier sphere inside our yellow house on the corner of Quaker Street. Our nation has fought in Panama, Haiti, Iraq (twice), Bosnia, Kosovo, Somalia, Afghanistan, and Kuwait. The country has had four presidents, economic expansions that induced euphoria, and economic busts that produced despair.

The Berlin Wall fell; the Soviet Union expired.

The cell phone was born; the rotary phone died—except in my mother-in-law's apartment, where a pair exist like endangered animals in a zoo. Someday they will be moved to the Smithsonian.

The number of stoplights between my home in Lincoln and downtown Burlington has climbed from six to nineteen. The number of Wal-Marts in Vermont has gone from zero to four. The dairy industry in Lincoln disappeared completely: It went extinct on an appropriately wet and gray day in December 1992 when Tom Densmore, the last dairy farmer in town, packed his herd into the trucks that would take the cows to the auction barn three hours away.

My wife and I have had two parents and three grandparents die. We've become parents ourselves. We've owned nine cats and four hermit crabs (so far, we have yet to lose a crab to a cat), and eight separate cars (though, thank heavens, never more than two at a time), including a used 1983 Colt we bought when we first moved to Vermont for $1,100. I drove that car until the passenger doors rusted shut and I had to climb into the vehicle through the hatch in the back.

Though I hadn't envisioned this column would become a diary, it's clear to me how it evolved into one: I was simply recording what was going on around me. Yes, I wrote about the cataclysmic terrorist attacks of September 11, 2001—when my wife was younger, she worked on the 104th floor of one of the World Trade Center towers—as well as what meaning might be found in my Armenian grandparents' bewildering courtship. I shared with my readers my Manhattan sister-in-law's fanatic determination to have a vegetable garden three hundred miles to the north, regardless of how much those carrots would cost her.

But on any given week I was more likely to chronicle my daughter's birth or my mother's death. Or the pleasure my neighbor Don Gale, an engineer by day, gets from boiling maple sap into syrup. Or the way Don's teenage daughter, Jennifer, memorialized her dead horse, Gumbo Tiger Lily C. The animal had to be put to sleep, and I will never forget what Jennifer's sobbing mother said to me after the veterinarian had euthanized the animal with a syringe the size of a thermos, and Jennifer was gently stroking the dead horse's broad but lifeless neck: "It's easy for her to be strong. She doesn't have to see her daughter's heart breaking."

I have learned so much from these people.

Perhaps because this is a book about a town, I have divided the columns into sections that reflect some of Lincoln's notable points of interest—or, perhaps, those parts of the village that I have always found most interesting. I have not dated the pieces, but they proceed roughly chronologically within each section.

That means, for example, that my daughter might be a fourth-grader in one group of columns and a toddler in the next. She does not, however, travel backward in time within any one section.

Likewise, careful readers will note that the number of dairy farms in Vermont in one case is 2,300, while in another it is closer to 1,600. The first reference is from 1993, the second from 2001. Make no mistake: The dairy farm is beleaguered in Vermont.

There are also occasional references to Bristol, the town next to Lincoln. It is a veritable metropolis compared to my modest hamlet, with a grocery store, a pharmacy, and a wonderful little bookstore. An eye-widening 4,000 people live there—four times the population of Lincoln.

Finally, not all of these columns appeared originally in the *Burlington Free Press.* The longer pieces appeared in the *Boston Globe,* most in that paper's Sunday magazine but some in the travel section or the opinion pages, too.

It would be hard to thank my neighbors for all that they have given my family and me over the years, but I hope this book— an inadvertently public diary—expresses a small measure of my profound affection.

THE
YELLOW HOUSE
ON THE CORNER OF
QUAKER STREET

NOW THAT THE COWS ARE GONE

THE SUN WOULDN'T rise for two more hours, but by 5:00 in the morning Tom Densmore was in the barn milking cows. When the trucks arrived shortly before 8:00—two the length of tractor trailers and a third perhaps half that long—he had finished milking the animals, but he hadn't begun to disassemble the feed carts or milking machines. That would have to wait until the afternoon.

It took Densmore and the truckers three hours to march his sixty-head herd up the metal ramps into the trucks, about what the thirty-four-year-old farmer had expected. By 11:30, the trucks were beginning their slow descent on the steep road that had led them up to the Vermont hill farm, winding past miles of new-growth forest, and then through the center of town, with its immaculate white church, general store, and two dozen village houses with sharply pitched roofs.

The animals arrived at the auction barn, about three hours away, in midafternoon. It took auctioneer Herb Gray less than ninety minutes to dispose of the herd, selling the milking cows one by one and some of the calves in small groups. Most of the cows brought Densmore $800 to $1,100 each, while the calves went for $200 to $700 apiece—not enough to pull him completely out of debt.

Densmore's mother, sister, and one of his brothers stood by him as his cows were scattered to farms across Vermont and New Hampshire. Nita, Nola, and Nicki—alliteration that signaled the cows were from the same family—were separated, as were three of Densmore's best producers: Kim, Amy, and Fayne. Every year they gamely produced well over 16,000 pounds of milk each.

Densmore's sixty-head herd was small even by Vermont standards, but it represented the last dairy farm in Lincoln, and the auction last December formally marked the end of an era. Lincoln, a village thirty miles southeast of Burlington, boasted forty-six active dairy farms as recently as 1945. Today there are none. There may be an occasional cluster of cows or beef cattle visible on the hillsides that roll throughout Lincoln, but there will be no more silver trucks from the Eastern Milk Producers Cooperative winding their way through town or trying to negotiate the narrow roads that link the homes in the hills.

Like many of Vermont's small rural towns, Lincoln has changed. In 1950, there were 11,019 dairy farms in Vermont. Today there are barely 2,300. The farms that remain are bigger—an average Vermont dairy farm has seventy-three milking cows, up from fifty-five as recently as 1978—and the cows produce more milk: roughly 15,500 pounds per cow per year these days, versus 11,500 pounds fifteen years ago.

Some of the farms disappeared simply because the farmers grew too old to milk fifty or sixty cows twice a day, and their children chose more lucrative occupations: carpentry or real estate or manufacturing jobs in Connecticut and Massachusetts. Other farmers got out when they discovered that while they may have been cash-poor, their land was valued by down-country immigrants: Selling a few acres a year might take care of the property taxes. And some farmers simply became frustrated by the economics of the industry. The price of milk today is unchanged from 1978, but the cost of producing that milk—everything from seed to the taxes on the land—has risen.

Some of the changes in Lincoln are immediately apparent: Meadows and pastures that once were farms have become forest. New homes have appeared in the past twelve months on both sides of the white clapboard building that houses the town clerk's office. Other changes may be harder to see, but they are no less significant: The three men and women who are Lincoln's selectmen this year are from Pittsburgh, Boston, and Grinnell, Iowa. One of them has lived in Lincoln barely two years.

What was once a largely self-contained community in which everyone worked his own land or was employed by one of the local mills that peppered the New Haven River, a community in which everyone knew how everyone else would vote at town meeting each March, has been transformed.

And it has been transformed, at least in part, by people like me. My wife and I discovered Lincoln in 1986. At the time we were living in Brooklyn, New York, in a modest apartment with windows that boasted bulletproof glass. She was a unit trust trader, and I was an advertising executive. We had grand visions of upward mobility, something we defined as a bigger apartment in a worse neighborhood. We knew the last names of most of our neighbors in the five-story brownstone in which we lived because we saw their names on the mailboxes, but we knew few first names, and rarely could we have matched a last name to a face.

At some point that spring, we decided to move to Vermont. I had never set foot in the state, and my wife hadn't been there since she spent a month at a summer camp near Lake Champlain. We had certainly never heard of a village called Lincoln.

But we had a shared vision of Vermont that drew us north: an image of green hills dotted with black-and-white Holsteins, an ethic of hard work that was symbolized for us by a mythic image of a barn lit before daybreak. We imagined villages in which everyone knew everyone's name and neighbors took care of one another. We imagined a place like Lincoln.

Lincoln sits in a valley midway up Mount Abraham, a 4,000-foot mountain, at an elevation of about 1,200 feet. Geography is destiny here. People do not stumble upon the town by accident or because they are driving between Burlington and Rutland. The center of Lincoln is located three miles off a two-lane road that continues thirty miles northwest into Burlington. The road to Lincoln coils uphill, twisting through rocky hills thick with maple and pine and ash.

Residents take pride in the town's isolation and in the fact that its growing season is ten days shorter than Bristol's, a village only four miles away but situated at a much lower elevation. Some years, there are midsummer frosts heavy enough to kill young pumpkins the size of softballs.

Mount Abraham, known once as Potato Hill, towers over Lincoln and is shaped more like a toppled peach than a potato. The population of the town is about 975 people, an increase of 100 residents since 1980 but still well below the 1,400 people who lived here a century ago. By the time my wife and I arrived in Lincoln, most of the dairy farms were already gone, but there were still enough cows that the place could be mistaken for a farming community by someone who didn't know better.

There were three dairy farmers in town in 1986. There was Tom Densmore, who was renting a hundred acres from Paul Goodyear, land that Paul and his wife, Wanda, had farmed since 1945. There was Herb Parker, with fifty cows and fifty heifers, who somehow managed to cut hay in fields steep enough for a ski slope. And there was Norman Strickholm, a man in his early thirties who was renting land for his cows from retired farmers Fletcher and Harriett Brown—land that, according to the Browns, Robert Frost had once offered to buy.

The road turns to dirt as it passes Paul and Wanda Goodyear's farm. It continues upward toward the Lincoln Gap and over the mountain to Warren, but it isn't plowed in the winter and becomes impassable sometime around Halloween. In the winter, the Goodyears really do live at the end of the road.

Paul Goodyear arrived in Lincoln in 1945, bringing with him ten cows and a pair of horses from Hancock, a town about one-third the size of Lincoln, on the other side of the mountain. He paid $1,600 for 167 acres, a farmhouse, and a barn. According to the town appraisal, his property is worth $209,000 today. For forty years Paul and Wanda ran a dairy farm in the shadow of Mount Abraham, usually with about fifty cows. Their farmhouse looks out on meadows that are already becoming overgrown with brush. "In 1945, the farms were everywhere," Paul Goodyear says. "Back then, most everybody had a few cows. People didn't go to Bristol or Burlington to work." The town had its own creamery, and there was a dairy only fifteen miles away in Starksboro.

While farms have been steadily disappearing in Vermont since the end of World War II, Goodyear witnessed most of Lincoln's farmers give up dairying in the early 1960s, when the milk can was replaced by the bulk tank. Instead of filling large cans with their milk, farmers were asked by the dairies to buy and install refrigerated tanks to store the milk so the handlers could pick it up in large tanker trucks.

"The biggest drop-off was probably 1963, when we all had to put in the bulk tanks," Goodyear says. "They cost $1,200, which was a lot of money back then, plus we had to build a new milk house for it. That cost another $2,000. I guess there were twenty or twenty-five of us farming here before bulk tanks. Only five of us decided to stay in after."

Now in their sixties and seventies, the Goodyears have no less affection for Lincoln than they had when they were young. But there are moments when they no longer recognize the town in which they raised six children. "We don't know each other as well as a community," Paul says. "We can't. People keep coming in, and we don't know who they are. There are more people in the choir now than there used to be in the whole church."

Thirty-five years ago, neighbors would visit the Goodyears' farmhouse without an invitation and stay for supper, which suited Wanda just fine. "Anyone would drop in for a meal, no one would feel a need to call ahead," she says. "It was wonderful. Of course, no one would dare do that now. They'd be embarrassed—or think it was an imposition."

At different times over the last five decades, Paul has been a selectman, an auditor, and the town fire warden. As the town has grown, he believes a volunteer ethic has been lost. "We were all for one and one for all. If anyone had a calamity, a whole gang would join in and solve the problem," he says, quickly citing two examples. When his corn silo blew down in a 1949 windstorm, he and a dozen friends built a new one within days; in the fall of 1961, when he broke an arm, fifteen neighbors descended upon his farm with tractors and chain saws and cut the wood his family would need for the winter.

The Goodyears stopped farming in 1985. Only one of their children was interested in farming, and he had already established a farm elsewhere. "It wasn't economical to farm, so most everyone went on to do other things," Wanda says. They were relieved when Tom Densmore, then in his mid-twenties, asked if he could rent their land; for seven more years their farm remained active and alive.

Herb Parker stands in the backyard of his farmhouse and sweeps his arm over the hillsides that surround him to the west, the north, and the east, and he ticks off names of families who own farms. "Buss. Reynolds. Perfect. Way up there: Goodyear. It's all forest now. But it used to be clear. It used to be mowed," he says. "I miss that. I miss those farms."

Parker and his wife, Lois, ran a dairy farm on land that had been in his family for more than a century. In 1987, well into their fifties, they sold their hundred-cow herd in the federal government's Whole Herd Buyout program—an attempt to boost milk prices by decreasing supply. Until that day, Parker boasts, he had gone thirty-four consecutive years without missing a milking. "The day after we sold the cows," he says, "we regretted it. It was fun not having them around for about a week, but then we started missing them. The days and nights seemed awfully long after we got rid of them."

Today the Parkers have the closest thing to a dairy-size herd left in Lincoln. They raise beef cattle and have up to a hundred animals on their farm at any one time. "But it's not like it once was," Herb says. "Dairy farming and sugaring used to tie us all together." Like the Goodyears, the Parkers feel like strangers in Lincoln's town center. "I go to town meetings now and I don't know most of the people," Herb says. Lois adds, "You feel like an outsider because there are so many out-of-state people."

The first real influx of out-of-state people arrived in Lincoln in the early 1970s, including a group of Middlebury College students who discovered the hill town sixteen miles northeast of the campus and started buying acres of cheap land. Some built geodesic domes or restored farmhouses. Some married, had children, and helped start a preschool.

Today there are still a half-dozen homes filled with these "alfalfa sprouts," as one elderly farmer describes them. One of them, Cynthia Price, is a nationally recognized painter who has spent a decade interpreting on canvas something she calls an "endangered species"—the barn. Her home is on the edge of what was once a thriving dairy farm run by James Moody, who stopped farming in the mid-'70s and died two years ago. "Jim's barns were so important to him. They're falling apart now," Price says, "but they're still incredibly beautiful."

A for-sale sign appeared in the yard by Moody's empty farmhouse in April, and Price fears that she's going to wake up one morning and find his barns gone, replaced by a housing development.

Like Herb Parker, James Moody subscribed to a rural aesthetic that prized field over forest. For a full decade after his animals were gone, he climbed onto his tractor and hayed his fields. Price says that some of her friends—"us flatlander hippies"— brought controversy to Lincoln: Their desire for a preschool may have been more controversial with the old-timers than the sight of young men with ponytails; their belief that the center elementary school had to be improved was almost insulting.

The elementary school was built by volunteer labor—farmers who found time between haying and milking—in 1952, after an earlier schoolhouse burned down. In 1978, when the proposal to establish a public kindergarten was rejected at a town meeting, the young parents who had been running a preschool in the town hall raised money to construct their own building.

Price says that while the old-timers may have occasionally smirked at the colony of Middlebury alumni and their friends, they tended to take individuals in the group under their wing. Kim Smith remembers buying land from a local building excavator, Floyd Hall, in 1972: "He could have really stuck it to me if he'd wanted to, but he didn't. I was this twenty-two-year-old college kid from the Midwest who had some money, and I had no idea what land was supposed to cost. But Floyd charged me what I've since come to realize was a fair price. It was the same way when he put in my driveway. He's just a real honest guy."

Even though he wears his hair long and brought vegetarian falafel burgers to the A & W in Middlebury after he bought the restaurant, Smith has been consistently elected to the town school board since the mid-1980s. There is often heated debate at town meetings about the rising cost of education, but "we've never had a school budget defeated," he says proudly. "This community has always been very supportive."

While the barns in the hills may be decaying, the center of town had a dramatic face-lift in the 1980s. "Downtown Lincoln wasn't so picturesque when I got here in the early 1970s," Price recalls.

When most Vermont towns are gentrified, the impetus—and the funding—is likely to come from newcomers. Lincoln is an exception. What Price calls the "beautification of the downtown" began with a tragedy and was led by families with Lincoln pedigrees dating back well into the last century.

In 1981, on the night of Good Friday, a gas leak in the United Church of Lincoln sparked a fire that reduced the only active church in town to ashes. About all that remained of the century-old Protestant church was the steel weathervane that rose from the top of the steeple. The church had rested on a small rise, at one of the four corners where Lincoln's two main roads intersect, the literal and metaphoric heart of the town. When Easter Sunday services were held that year at the town hall, diagonally across the street from the hillside where the church had been, the parishioners looked out windows toward the still smoldering ashes, and many of them wept.

Rev. David Wood and his wife, Donna, had arrived in town only two years earlier, and were still getting to know the congregation when the church went up in flames. They were a couple in their late twenties with two young children. "A lot of people thought David would just turn around and leave when the church burned," Donna says. "But I knew he wouldn't. I knew *we* wouldn't."

About half a mile from the center of town was the old Methodist church building, which for decades had stood vacant. While it might have been easier to simply rededicate the church for ecumenical Protestant services, the fire had left a hole in the center of town more pronounced than the loss, perhaps, of a whole city block in the middle of Boston.

"Imagine driving up the road to Lincoln and finding that hill empty," says Beverly Brown. Brown grew up beside the church and owned the general store across the street with her husband, Donald, for almost fifteen years.

The congregation raised the money it needed to move the old Methodist church a half-mile, drop it in place on the hillside, and restore it. The effort cost $164,000—and thousands of hours in volunteer labor. While half of the money came from insurance, another half was raised by the congregation through venison suppers, bake sales, and hundreds of letters requesting grants and private donations.

Bill Finger, who spent summers in Lincoln as a boy and moved to the town permanently in 1974, recalls, "That fire galvanized the church and the community. A lot of people still feel it was an act of God that in the long run brought a lot of people together."

The congregation completed the restoration of the church in 1983, and, motivated by what Paul and Wanda Goodyear's daughter Linda Norton describes as "the desire to give something back," a second restoration project was begun. A group of parishioners raised money to buy two houses across the street from the church, one on the verge of collapse, and convert them to use as affordable housing for the community's elderly. Today, the housing complex consists of ten separate apartments in three buildings, all of which look like well-kept private homes.

That project cost $250,000—not including volunteer carpentry, wallpapering, and painting—and transformed the four corners that comprise Lincoln center into the sort of idyllic picture postcard that entices advertising executives and unit trust traders away from New York.

Cynthia Price's nightmare—waking up to find the barns next door replaced by a development—could happen. But it's not likely. The town has safeguards to prevent such things. With the exception of the apartments for the elderly, the town does not allow new homes to be constructed on lots smaller than one acre.

But as the farmers sell off their land, there is no question that houses do appear. Ivis and Stewart Masterson farmed in South

Lincoln for three decades before calling it quits in 1968. At one point they owned 275 acres. Today they own less than two. "We started selling off the land thirty years ago, and people started building houses," Ivis says. "There are so many more people now." At least fourteen houses dot the land that was once the Masterson farm. Adjacent to that land is an eight-house development.

Although the first influx of out-of-state people was hippies, the second influx was young professionals who chose not to settle in cities. Flatlanders like my wife and me began arriving in the 1980s; many of them now commute to Burlington or Middlebury or Vergennes.

Karen Lueders and her husband, Jim DuMont, are both attorneys. She is from Boston, he is from New York City, and they are raising their three children in a farmhouse near land that until recently Norman Strickholm was maintaining as one of the two active dairy farms in Lincoln.

"Everything that happened to us here was touched by kindness," Lueders says, recalling 1986, her family's first year in Lincoln. When part of the roof blew off their house one Christmas when they were gone, their neighbors immediately repaired it; when they failed to make arrangements to have their long driveway plowed before the first blizzard, Strickholm cleared the snow at no charge.

Lueders would take her young children and wander to the farm to watch Strickholm milk his Ayrshire cows. In 1991, Strickholm moved his herd to Colorado, where land is cheaper and where he thought dairying would be more profitable. "Norman's leaving was traumatic for our family," Lueders says. "Just knowing he was out there milking the cows was a part of our life."

Like Strickholm, Ivis Masterson farmed Lincoln's rocky soil, and she understands why none of her five children chose to continue the family's dairy tradition: "They knew the hardship of our lives. They knew there was little money. All five of the kids have a better life than we had."

Although Masterson misses the quiet farm life, she appreciates that many newcomers contribute to the community: "I know there's an awful lot of young people out there who've come here and tied this place together the way we once did with the farms." The Mastersons did not sell all of their land; they gave some of it to their children who have remained in town.

Four of the Mastersons' five children stayed in Lincoln, an important dynamic in a town bonded in part by multigenerational families. All of Donald and Beverly Brown's three sons have remained, as has Fletcher and Harriett Brown's daughter.

"Unlike suburbia, where there are whole neighborhoods of people the same age, there are a lot of different generations within each family still here in Lincoln," Beverly Brown says. At any moment on a Sunday morning in church, it is possible for me to see a host of Browns: Jim and Judy, as they sing in the choir; Harriett, a deacon, passing the offering plate along the pews; Beverly, tracking down a cassette tape of the service so that the elderly who can't make it to church are able to hear what they missed; and brothers Fletcher and Donald, deep in conversation before the bells have rung and called them to their pews, discussing, perhaps, the spring sugar run.

I am always moved when I see the Browns together in church —more now than seven years ago, when I failed to understand the complex blood network that links one of Lincoln's first families. I never went to church in Brooklyn, and I started attending in Lincoln only when Fletcher Brown commented on the fact that my house and the church share the same driveway. Noting my unique proximity to the sanctuary—forty yards, closer than the parsonage—Fletcher said, in his wry and unmistakably understated voice, "Don't have much of an excuse not to go to church now, do you?"

Shame first brought me there, but fellowship and faith have led me to stay.

The farms may have left Lincoln, but the sense of community hasn't. There is no question that the town has changed, that the influx of new people has transformed a once self-contained rural community into something vaguely suburban. Each weekday morning, a lot of Lincoln winds its way down the road that milk tankers once took, and I wouldn't be surprised to find a stoplight someday where the road to Lincoln meets the road to Burlington.

Clearly the town lost something when it lost its farms, but sometimes I'm not sure it lost anything more substantial than cows. That sounds glib, but it may also be true. Alice Leeds teaches fifth and sixth grade at the elementary school. She has taught in rural communities in the South; she has taught in midtown Manhattan. Inspired this spring by the case of the Chicago parents who left their two young children home alone while they took a Caribbean vacation, Leeds devoted class time to the ethical issues of leaving children unsupervised. What her students told her surprised her.

"Most of the kids—two-thirds—said they're never scared when they're home alone," Leeds says. "People feel responsible for each other here, and the kids understand that Lincoln is their place. They're comfortable here, they feel safe here."

If I worried for Lincoln's soul, those concerns were eased at the funeral service this May for Tari Shattuck, a forty-one-year-old neighbor who died of leukemia. Shattuck was born in Paris and raised in Texas. She arrived in Lincoln in 1972, a Democrat in a Republican hill town. Among the women and men who spoke at her service—at which every seat was filled and some mourners had to view the eulogy on video monitors set up in the Sunday-school classrooms—was Fred Thompson.

Thompson's Lincoln roots date back to the nineteenth century. He is a conservative Yankee, tough at town meetings, skeptical of most budget initiatives. He served with Shattuck on the town planning commission in the early 1980s, a fact I never knew until he began to speak at the front of the church on the day of her funeral.

"If any of you want to know how much Tari Shattuck loved this town, how much she cared for all of you, go to the town clerk's office and take a look at the town plan she wrote," Thompson said, and then his voice broke abruptly. He might have planned to say more, but if he did he changed his mind, and he started back to his seat. "A flaming liberal!" he said, shaking his head in mock disgust, and I saw some of her family smile through their tears.

I had found a seat in the choir loft before the service began, so I had the opportunity to see a lot of faces that afternoon: aging hippies with beards and bad neckties, some of the women in peasant skirts; elderly farmers wiping their eyeglasses; teachers from the local school; selectmen past and present; choir members sitting for once in the pews. I saw Goodyears and Nortons and Browns; I saw three generations of families scattered across the church like wildflower seeds.

I saw more of the town together than I've seen even at a town meeting. I saw Lincoln, once again, looking out for its own.

SOWING THE SEEDS
WITH A LITTLE SPROUT

IN THE NEXT two weeks, I will plant the seeds for my snow peas. In soil rich in compost I will mold beds from dark earth, and into those beds I will tuck the small light green—khaki-colored, really—marbles that with any luck will be robust, flowering plants soon after Memorial Day.

It is the peas that come first in this garden. I plant them with my hands and one tool: a hoe I purchased at a lawn sale eight years ago for exactly one dollar.

That day when snow peas go into the ground is one of my favorite days of the year, an hour-long chore that I extend—methodically, but joyfully—into a two-hour ritual. It is, for me, my own personal May Day.

It is not the May Day of labor rallies—although gardening is certainly about labor, and the fruits and vegetables thereof—but the May Day that celebrates something more primal. Rebirth. Renewal. The reassurance that we have survived another winter, no small accomplishment here in Vermont.

That's why I use few tools and no gloves: I want to be, literally, in my garden. I want to feel dirt on my hands.

Some years, my peas may go into the ground as early as today, April 24; some years, I may have to wait until Mother's Day. My May Day is hostage to climate, not calendar.

This spring, the ritual will be especially meaningful. For the first time I will have a child with me, a little girl who will be a few weeks short of six months when I plant. The ritual this year will feel different because I will have with me an audience of one, sitting in something called a Summer Seat: a canvas chair with a back designed to support a small baby's back and spine.

During my own private May Day last year my wife was pregnant, but the distance between expectation and parenthood was as incomprehensible as the chasm that exists between a seed and a plant. I am always amazed at the way the seeds I grasp in one closed fist can become a flowering row of bushes thirty feet long and three feet high.

In my fantasy, the ritual will begin this year not with the moment I tear open a packet of seeds, but when I place my daughter in her chair at the edge of the garden. In my mind's eye, one of her hands is in her mouth, the other is pulling at the cuff of her sweater. Her feet, in tiny corduroy slippers, touch the grass.

She watches me as I work, her eyes wide, and because she is watching I may decrease the time the ritual takes—a small concession to an attention span that is short. But it is also possible that this first planting may take even longer, as I pause to explain to her exactly what I'm doing, placing her on one of my knees as I show her dirt and seed and hoe.

My parents never gardened, and so I'm sometimes surprised that it has become for me such a passion. I like vegetables, but it is the act of gardening itself that I love. I have no idea if my daughter will share this interest, if she, too, will derive satisfaction from planting and watering and pulling the damned from the ground so that the chosen may prosper. On one level, I hope that she does.

But on another level, I know if she gardens with me my May Days will become clouded with the annual recognition that she is growing up and I am growing old. Last year she was in utero, this year she is in a Summer Seat. Next year she will be walking, and the year after that she may want to help: How many seeds can a two-and-a-half-year-old hide in her fist?

I expect I will learn. And I know I will be moved.

THAT ROOF DIDN'T COLLAPSE: IT'S A HOME IMPROVEMENT PROJECT

I JUST CAME off the roof. Again.

I'm thinking of putting a tent up there and staying until June. I've never been a private person, but remaining on the roof might be easier than hauling the thirty-two-foot extension ladder through three-and-a-half feet of snow from the barn to the house on a daily basis.

Like many Vermonters, I've spent a fair amount of time this year—and, yes, this past week—shoveling snow off the roof. The other day I shoveled or used the snow rake to pull snow off the roof over the front door, the roof over the screen porch, the roof over the glass porch, and the roof over the back of the barn, the walls of which already are bowing like the letter "C" on *Sesame Street*.

This winter Vermonters have had two approaches to all that snow on our houses and barns. There has been the approach taken by my friends Greg Vitercik and Carol Murray of Lincoln, which has been to use the snow as a home improvement tool:

They planned to remove the decaying, old carriage barn by their house this summer, but decided instead to let the piles of snow do the dirty work and drive the old structure into the ground.

My wife was actually there the morning when the mountains of snow finally caused the mass of tired wood to groan, sag, and then collapse in slow motion. It reminded her of the way ocean liners always sink in the movies, sliding slowly underwater with the grace of a dolphin.

Next up for the Murray-Viterciks is replacing the floor of their front porch. It sags pretty badly, so Greg asked if I'd mind sending some of that snow I took off my roof his way. He believes he needs just a little more weight to turn the porch into Pompeii and make its recovery an architectural dig.

On the other hand, some of us—including yours truly—have been removing the snow from our roofs with more energy than we have ever put into a real job. There have been whole afternoons (and evenings) when I didn't write a single word, because I was too busy pounding at the ice jams in the valleys of my roofs, and figuring out new ways to approach the ice at the peaks.

The purpose of all this activity was not simply because I would rather stand on a slippery porch roof in the snow at seven at night than write, or even because I feared this old house was about to become a Bob Vila restoration special. It was because the snow and ice was actually melting, and it was melting right into the kitchen and the front hall.

There have been times this winter when I've had to be a very determined and clever lad. One time I was standing on a porch roof about fifteen feet off the ground, banging away with a hatchet at the bottom edge of a two-foot-thick glacier coming down a valley in the roof above the attic and the second floor. I had surrounded myself with the snow I'd pulled off the higher roof so that if I fell I would merely fall into the snow on the porch roof, and not onto the ground.

Sure enough I slipped and fell right into that snow, which (thank you very much) did indeed prevent me from falling into the yard.

Then, of course, the hatchet—which I had tossed reflexively into the air when I slipped—came crashing down and conked me on the head.

Fortunately I was hit by the blunt end, so I am (as my wife observed) "neither disfigured nor dead."

Although this snow has been hard work, I'll miss it when it's gone—especially since it will leave behind rivers of mud when it melts.

On the other hand, all that mud won't wind up on my roof. At least I don't think it will. After this winter, I probably shouldn't be too sure about anything.

LOVE BLOOMS OVER THE SEPTIC TANK

MY WIFE IS an incurable romantic, and so for our thirteenth wedding anniversary she wanted our septic tank pumped.

There were other things she wanted too, of course. She's not insane. But a freshly pumped septic tank was top of the list, because in her opinion an ounce of prevention is worth seventeen tons of septic tank overflow on your bathroom floor, or in your backyard, or wherever it is that four years of flushing will go when there's no more room at the inn.

And so a few days before our wedding anniversary in October, I ventured gamely outside, my shovel in one hand and a map in the other. The map had the precise location of the septic tank.

I'd made the map myself, which should have been a pretty good indication that it wouldn't be long before I'd be informing Mission Control we had a problem. But the arrows and numbers looked accurate, and the landmarks seemed in the right spots: The mountain ash, the corner of the house, the outdoor spigot for the hose.

More important, I remembered my resolve when I'd made the map four years ago, after losing our septic tank for the second time in a decade. I'd spent a day digging and dowsing (yes, dowsing), and failed to find anything more valuable than a garden trowel.

With the resolve of Scarlett O'Hara at the end of the first half of *Gone With the Wind,* I'd stood that day at sunset with a clump of dirt in my hand, and vowed I would never, ever misplace our humanure humidor again.

Well, I was wrong. I did.

I wasn't quite as pathetic a spectacle this time as I was four years ago: Then I'd had to randomly dig holes throughout the backyard, and still I'd accomplished little more than the creation of a scale model of the mountains and valleys that bisect our state. Eventually, we'd had to wait for the snow to fall and melt before we could find that all-important patch of warm earth above the poop pantry.

This time I knew more or less where the tank was, and after about an hour of digging I actually hit the cement roof. I did not, however, hit the lid. I did not grab that all-important brass (wrought-iron, to be precise) ring.

But I was nevertheless savoring no small amount of satisfaction: Even if my map was in error, even if I was off by a few feet, I had still made progress in my quest to become a competent homeowner. Whereas a half-decade ago I had managed to misplace a whole septic tank, this time I had only managed to lose the lid.

The problem—and I tried to convince myself that *problem* was way too strong a word—was that I wasn't sure in which direction I should dig to find the lid. Moreover, I hadn't a clue whether the septic tank was eight or eighteen feet long, or whether it was shaped like a rectangle or a square.

And so I started to shovel. I dug toward the house, driven by a vague recollection that I was standing near the far side of the tank.

I didn't find the ring right away, but it didn't take long before I found a second edge—which meant I actually had two sides of the tank. Even a geometry-challenged goober like me can find a septic tank top when you have two sides of the box.

And, thank you very much, soon enough I did, indeed, unearth the lid.

It wasn't the most romantic of anniversary presents, and it certainly wasn't aromatic. But it was exactly what my lovely bride wanted, and far be it from me to deny her the peace of mind that comes with a spanking clean doody bin.

SCENIC BARN IS REALLY A SCRAPYARD

MY BARN IS a biohazard. OK; maybe that's harsh. And imprecise. My barn makes an auto graveyard look like a playground for preschoolers.

I discovered this during Labor Day weekend, when I made the mistake of cleaning it. A friend of mine was about to begin repairs on the barn so it didn't sink so deep into the earth that I could no longer park a Chevy Cavalier inside it, and he'd suggested that I move everything from the back of the barn to the front.

The floor at the back of the barn is made of wood. The floor at the front is made of cement.

That means the front is a downright suburban two-car garage, while the back is a magnificent and fascinating collection of horse stalls, corn cribs and feeding troughs. There's hay back there from the Hoover administration.

Over the last half-century, the back of the barn served two purposes: It was used by roaming cats as a truck stop, and it was used by people for storage.

A little over a decade ago, when my wife and I moved to Lincoln, we added a third use: transfer station. Whenever we had something useless that was big or metal or merely frighteningly toxic, we hauled it off to the back of the barn. Old empty paint cans went there to die.

Our intent, usually, was to bring the debris to the dump come Saturday morning. The problem? Until my wife's recent acquisition of her spacious, powerful, and deeply suburban minivan, we always drove very small vehicles. Sunbirds. Colts. Cavaliers.

Have you ever tried to get the metal frame to a sixty-two-inch-long storm window into a 1983 Plymouth Colt? It's not a pretty sight, especially since we had four of those storm windows to take to the dump one Saturday, and every single one of them had dangling shards of glass.

So we gave up and hauled them into the back of the barn.

Same fate for the rusty metal gate we took down in the backyard. That gate is ten feet long and four feet high, and it's a tetanus shot waiting to happen.

The embarrassing thing is that eventually everything my wife and I couldn't deal with wound up in the back of the barn. When I cleaned it out, I found tires and spares from cars we no longer own (a total of seventeen tires), roughly forty feet of metal gutter (much of it speckled with house paint), and easily two hundred books too horrible to donate to the Lincoln Library (a library that lost eighty percent of its collection in this summer's flood).

Just how ridiculous are the books back there? They range from a waterlogged poetry anthology that I bought in the fourth grade because the cover was an image from a lavishly produced movie version of Tennyson's *The Charge of the Light Brigade,* to a few volumes of the antiquarian *Messages and Papers of the Presidents,* each of which has been saturated with feral cat pee.

While some presidential missives might be improved by the stench of cat urine—especially the ones between presidents and their interns—my sense is that James Madison deserved better.

What else is back there? No fewer than seventy-five plastic flowerpots, two massive wooden barrels—one of which is filled with the bobbins the Lincoln mill once produced, and one of which is now the home to our two broken mailboxes—and fifty-six ancient wooden shutters.

Whenever someone in Lincoln sneezes, flecks of paint fly off those shutters, and the air must be filled with lead chips and mercury. Those shutters are old, and that paint is very scary.

Consequently, later this fall I will bite the bullet and borrow a pickup, and haul the rubble to the dump. I'll air out those books, and cart the ones that can be salvaged to the library. And while the cats will miss their bookstore-cum-urinal, at least they won't have to fight for space in the corn crib with a paint can.

DEAD CLUSTER FLIES SERVE AS WINDOW INSULATION FOR THE INEPT

I AM IN the midst of an important experiment. I'm testing to see if dead frozen cluster flies seal a window as well as weather stripping.

Like many theories, I came upon my idea that cluster flies might serve as window insulation entirely by chance. I made my annual December trek to the attic to press my Mortite brand caulking cord around the two windows up there and discovered—lo and behold—that there were so many dead, frozen cluster flies around the frame and midsection that the windows didn't rattle in their frames. I would have needed a garden trowel to get down to the bottom sash.

Consequently, I took my coils of Mortite and went back down the stairs.

Now a lot of guys would have had their houses securely sealed for the winter by mid-December, but I'm not a lot of guys when it comes to home maintenance. A toddler with a plastic hammer is more competent than I am when it comes to keeping a house standing.

In all fairness, I had caulked the first- and second-floor windows by Thanksgiving, but I avoid the attic like it's a big petri dish filled with the Ebola virus. It's cold and messy, and there are exposed nails that extend down from the ceiling timbers like icicles and rise up from the floorboards like stalagmites.

Some months of the year, it also houses a pretty wide array of wildlife. Sometimes there are mice, and sometimes there is something considerably larger: Based on the stomping, I'd guess it's either Barney the big purple dinosaur or an Olympic wrestler in clogs.

One time a bat flew out when my wife opened the door. In August there are hornets.

And, often, of course, there are cluster flies.

In any case, I hate venturing up there, which is why I never insulate the attic windows until mid-December.

This is the first time in a decade and a half, however, that I got up there so late into the heating season that the cluster flies had frozen to death. I must confess, I suspected something was different the moment I opened the door and didn't hear the familiar drone of several hundred thousand bugs flying headfirst into window glass, window frames, and each other.

When I saw what had occurred, briefly I considered getting a spatula and prying the frozen mess away from the sills and then vacuuming up the corpses, but my wife said we only had one vacuum bag left and it was clear to us both that I was going to need a half-dozen at the very least.

And so I did the next best thing. Nothing.

Then I got a thermometer and hung it smack in the center of the attic. It reads forty-four degrees as I write. I have been taking the temperature once a week, and I will have an average by the end of winter. At the same time, I am keeping a journal of the temperature outside on my front porch.

In the spring, when the cluster flies thaw, I will remove them. Then next fall, before the cold has arrived in earnest, I will caulk the attic windows with Mortite. No cluster flies this time. I'll use the good stuff.

Once again, I will monitor the temperature both inside my attic and outside on the porch, so I will have a sense of how the coming winter has differed from this one. In the end, I believe, I will know whether I should bother to caulk those attic windows or simply depend upon what just might be nature's own brand of insulation: the dead frozen cluster fly.

I'll keep you posted.

CITY SLICKER GETS A TASTE OF COUNTRY MARKETING

IN THE COUNTRY, roadblocks are not uncommon. You're driving through a small town, you've just passed the local firehouse, and suddenly there's a man in a uniform with a bucket asking for change. A quarter, a dime, whatever is sitting at that moment on your dashboard.

In some ways, it is the countryside's equivalent to the urban tactic of cleaning the windshields of stopped cars at traffic lights.

This is called a coin drop, and it is a critical fund-raising tool for the volunteer fire companies of many Vermont villages.

Except mine. For a coin drop to be successful, you need traffic, and Lincoln has precious little of that. You can't, so to speak, get anywhere from here.

Consequently, the members of the Lincoln Volunteer Fire Company have resorted to a more creative form of fund-raising: marketing.

And they're really quite good at it. I know this because I decimated a relatively strong ego by trying to help.

One Sunday afternoon the March before last, my neighbor stopped by my house holding about a dozen small fish in a net.

"Smelt," Rudy called them, and he asked me if I were a "smelt" man.

I'm not, but I didn't want to hurt his feelings since clearly the fish were for me. So I told him I'd never met a smelt I didn't like.

The fish were something like a bribe, and by accepting them I became the first official marketing director for the Lincoln Firemen's Barbecue Baste—famous in Lincoln for more than fifteen years and ready now to take Vermont by storm.

Of course it wasn't called the Lincoln Firemen's Barbecue Baste back then. Then it was simply The Sauce—an oil and vinegar concoction that had been doused liberally on chickens for more than fifteen years at the volunteer fire company's annual fund-raising barbecue.

Now I wasn't altogether sure what was involved with being marketing director for a local fire company's barbecue sauce. Although I had no delusions that the job would involve complex taste-tests against Kraft, or managing an advertising budget as large as General Motors', I wasn't sure what was expected. After all, it's no small task to take what is essentially a backyard barbecue sauce and bottle it—especially with nothing but volunteer labor. So I asked Rudy what being marketing director meant.

It meant, he said, making a label.

So I said yes.

But I was sure I could do more for Rudy than merely make a label, and I was sure the fire company could use the help. To get some insight into the sauce itself, I asked Rudy if he would be interested in my putting together a small research focus group of volunteers to explore the taste: what people liked about the product, and what—if anything—they disliked.

Rudy didn't think this was especially critical. "People seem to like the taste of it just fine," he told me. "We've used it at the barbecue every summer for fifteen years, and we haven't had a piece of leftover chicken yet."

I couldn't argue with that.

But then the very next day I wandered over to Rudy's house, and said helpfully, "This is a food product you have here, Rudy, and that means you need to get approval from certain groups— like the FDA." He nodded and pulled from an envelope a very important-looking piece of paper from something called the Agricultural Experiment Station at the University of Vermont. And then in a notebook he found for me some even more official-looking stationery from the Food and Drug Administration's Department of Health and Human Services. It seems they had already approached the FDA.

Still determined to provide Rudy with invaluable marketing guidance, I stopped by his house that weekend when I saw him out by his chicken coop. (He swears those birds have no idea that he has anything at all to do with a chicken barbecue sauce.) I wanted to talk to him about distribution, and why we should approach supermarkets. Think big, I told him, think big.

Rudy listened patiently to me (Rudy always listens patiently to me), and then explained that he thought distribution was under control. Jeff was talking with Grand Union, Bill and Dave were coordinating the efforts with the small general stores and "mom and pops," and he would be meeting with A&P the following week.

Undaunted, I brought up the subject of bottling. I said I knew a fellow in St. Johnsbury who might be able to help. Rudy nodded, and told me that the fire company was getting together over at the town hall for a few nights later in the month to bottle the first hundred cases. They would be bottling the baste in the dining room right below the auditorium. Claude, who owns the Lincoln General Store, had arranged everything: the vats, the ingredients, the production line.

Yup, Rudy said, the best thing I could do right now would be to come up with a real handsome label.

So I tried. I sat down for an evening or two and worked out all of the legal logistics, came up with a list of names, and then met one Wednesday night with the Lincoln Volunteer Fire Company's formal "Sauce Committee." Originally we considered naming the sauce Chief Bob's Barbecue Baste because we liked the alliteration (although we didn't use that word), and because our fire chief really is named Bob. But one of the committee members pointed out that it wasn't Bob's recipe, and besides, it was a project of the whole fire company. So we settled instead on the Lincoln Firemen's Barbecue Baste. It was longer, but we all felt pretty good about the name because—"from a marketing perspective"—we were suggesting in the brand name that it was a product from a nonprofit group. Plus, no one in the fire company could possibly feel left out.

The next step was to write the copy for the label and design some artwork. Someone wanted a drawing of a barbecued chicken breast, and someone else wanted a drawing of a fire helmet. One of the committee members suggested combining the two ideas: a chicken (albeit a living one) wearing a fire helmet and a barbecue apron. Although I figured I could write the copy just fine, I knew I'd need some help designing the artwork. I called on Reed, a friend of mine up the road who just happens to be one of Vermont's finest illustrators.

I told him the volunteer fire company needed a chicken. Now one of Reed's brothers-in-law is the fire chief, and another is the fire company's volunteer accountant. So I shouldn't have been surprised when Reed took me into his living room and showed me some of the sketches he had already worked up.

"Something like this?" he asked, showing me a drawing of a rather robust chicken wearing an apron and fire helmet, and holding a barbecue basting brush. "Yup," I said, not unduly concerned with the somewhat cannibalistic nature of the concept, "something like that."

And so we had a label. And two or three weeks later, we had a couple of thousand printed labels. And a week after that, in plenty of time for the first Memorial Day barbecues, we had a hundred bottled cases.

That was more than a year ago, and in that year the barbecue baste has done all right for itself: It can be found in a pretty fair number of grocery stores around the state, and the original recipe has been preserved ("makes just about everything from chicken to steak finger-Lincoln good"). And from my perspective, I have learned that when someone from Lincoln's library, or craft shop, or historical society asks me to be the "marketing director," I should simply smile, say sure, and be flattered that they have included me in their project at all.

THEATER, ON STAGE AND OFF, INSPIRES YOUNG ACTRESS

FEMALE BOXERS Laila Ali and Tonya "Tabloid-fare" Harding have nothing to fear from my nine-year-old daughter.

Last month I taught her how to make a fist and throw a punch. This was, in hindsight, a case of the blind leading the blind, because I've never punched anyone in my life, either. Once I hit a mailbox, but that was when I was seventeen and it was with my parents' car.

In any case, I knelt in our den, and I asked her to make a fist and take a swing. It wasn't pretty. She reminded me a bit of the head guy from the Munchkin City Lollipop Guild. This probably shouldn't have surprised me because my daughter's interests have always tended toward dancing and dolls—not boxing or athletics. This is a child who as recently as last autumn had to be told by the school gym teacher that after her foot (much to the astonishment of everyone present) actually whacked the big rubber orb in a game of kickball, she was supposed to run to first base.

She curled her thumb so that it was beside her index finger— five digits lined up in a row—rather than blanketed over her index and middle fingers. Then she flailed at the air like a toddler struggling for balance. I offered her my upper arm to whack, and after a few minutes, she was capable of delivering what I considered a reasonably authentic stage punch. It was never going to inflict serious damage, but at least it looked right.

I was proud of her, and not simply because she's so gentle that she hasn't the slightest idea how to inflict physical violence on anyone. I was pleased because the reason for this bizarre tutorial was an upcoming callback audition she had for the Vermont Stage Company's May production of *To Kill a Mockingbird,* and she was endeavoring to transform herself into that iconic tomboy named Scout. My daughter is many things, but she will never be mistaken off stage for a tomboy.

On stage? Maybe someday—though, sadly, not with this production.

But what is wonderful about my daughter's interest in drama —and it is more of an all-consuming, night-and-day passion than a mere interest—is the opportunity it has given the two of us to share something that I had never expected would link us together: theater.

My daughter is, clearly, going to be a drama jock. This also means, alas, that she is in for a world of rejection. I remember telling her last year when she did not get the part of Gretl in the Lyric Theatre's production of *The Sound of Music* that the disappointing news here wasn't this one rebuff: It was the reality that if she wanted to act, this rejection would be the first of many.

Her commitment to drama also means that we have savored together an extensive litany of musicals performed in area high schools and theaters, and a glorious few on Broadway. We have watched teenagers play Wendy and Peter Pan (and then dissected their performances), and speculated aloud upon what Reba McEntire was feeling when we saw her in her last week as Annie Oakley.

Moreover, it has added an unexpected depth to books we've cherished when we've seen them brought to the stage. When we are in the audience for the Lyric's *The Secret Garden* next month, we will see a new Victorian orphan girl named Mary Lennox: This one will sing of her sudden faith in the earth. We will meet a different grieving widower named Archibald Craven: This Craven's ardor for his late wife results in some of Broadway's more poignant love songs. When we see *To Kill a Mockingbird* in May, we will meet an Atticus Finch who almost certainly will broaden our image of Harper Lee's softspoken moral compass.

And in all the auditions, the callbacks, the successes and disappointments, there is the opportunity to read together, to think together, and, once in a while, to do something wondrously silly like learn how to throw a solid stage punch.

TWO TYPES OF WRITING

I'VE BEEN WRITING essays for this newspaper every Sunday morning for years, and I have always tried to separate the novelist from the columnist.

The only time that I can recall acknowledging in this space that I happen to write books was when one of my earlier novels, *Past the Bleachers,* was being filmed for a movie, and the ironies that surrounded the production were impossible to ignore. My favorite? Among the hundreds of people who were involved in the hard work of transforming a novel into a movie, I met two who had actually read the book.

I'm not precisely sure why I insisted on keeping the novelist out of my library when I was writing these columns, but I have a sense there were a number of reasons—some more prosaic than others.

I know, for example, that I never wanted to exploit the great gift of this space to sell my books. I never wanted to risk losing a reader because Sunday morning seemed to have become a commercial for a specific novel.

I know also that there has to be a Berlin Wall separating fiction and journalism—even fiction and the incoherent babble I sometimes offer about my chimney fires or my cats. Sometimes a person will ask me whether, for example, my friend Rudy once really climbed onto my roof with me in a blizzard to unblock an ice jam. It always gives me great pleasure to answer he did.

For better or worse, I really have had all those chimney fires. The Christmas tree really did once fall on my daughter. And I really do take her into the ladies' rooms in airports when we travel.

I don't make this stuff up.

My novels, of course, are another story. I make up every word. As far as I know, there isn't a ski resort in New England that depended upon a half-dozen female dowsers to halt a drought and bring rain . . . and thereby resurrect a river the resort needed to make snow. I'm not aware of a couple in Vermont who adopted a little boy whose father might once have played baseball for the Boston Red Sox. And I have never met a midwife who performed a cesarean section on a woman in a bedroom.

But there are other, more personal reasons for the way I have compartmentalized my professional life. I usually write my column on Friday afternoons, and I am usually writing for a Sunday a month in the future. I write this column at the very end of what we call the workweek, and I write it as a respite from the notion that I am in the midst of a book that will take many more months to complete, and no one will see for, perhaps, years.

I write it because it allows me to leave, for an afternoon, the complexities of creating a grieving parent or a lobbyist with no soul or a midwife on trial for manslaughter. It's not about escapism; writing about my mother's death may have been therapeutic, but it certainly wasn't an avoidance of reality. It is, however, an opportunity to simply be me: the guy who lives next door to the church and hasn't yet figured out how to ignite the pilot light on his furnace.

At 5:00 P.M. Monday, Vermont will be featured on *The Oprah Winfrey Show,* and a part of the program will focus on my current novel, *Midwives.* This will always be among the very greatest blessings I will ever receive, and someday I will figure out how to thank everyone involved.

For now, however, I want to be sure to thank all of you who have written me letters or baked me cookies or casseroles or the single best apple pie I've ever tasted. I've consumed the food, and now I will get to your letters. I promise.

And next week I will, once again, chronicle those other issues that matter to us all on a daily basis: School funding. The Southern Connector. The fact that I have, somehow, managed to lose my septic tank yet again.

THE
CENTER OF TOWN

LOSING THE LIBRARY

ON A SUMMER night in 1666, six years before she died, poet Anne Bradstreet watched her home in North Andover burn to the ground, taking with it one of the larger libraries in the New World. Publicly, at least, she approached its destruction with a combination of Puritan stoicism and faith, and bid farewell to the collection in a poem. Privately, was she somewhat less poised? I've always imagined she was, especially when she considered the ruination of all those books.

Lately, I've wondered as well how deeply her neighbors felt the loss of that library. I've envisioned them sifting through the black ashes in their black clothing and finding a charred spine from a book. A blistered cover. A flyleaf, singed along the edges.

This is, of course, conjecture. But despite the fact that she was a woman and that there were certainly leaders in her small world who frowned on her writing, I believe that Anne Bradstreet must have shared her impressive collection with her friends. If so, when she lost her library, her community would have felt the loss, too.

This summer, my small Vermont village lost its library. A hill town of roughly a thousand people, Lincoln sits in a valley midway up one of Vermont's highest peaks, the 4,052-foot Mount Abraham.

In the early morning hours of June 27, swollen by weeks of rain and four inches on the night of the 26th, the usually lazy New Haven River overran its banks and pummeled the town. No one was hurt, perhaps because the waters crested between 1:30 and 4:30 in the morning, so the roads along the river were quiet. But the rushing waters carved chasms in adjacent paved streets—one hole was an astonishing forty-five feet wide and thirty feet deep—and swept away steel and cement bridges that had stood for decades. Homes beside the river were flooded, and the banks were narrowed: Houses once ten to fifteen feet from the edge were now within thirty-six inches.

And though huge chunks of paved roads were chewed away and a pivotal bridge was destroyed, without question the greatest public casualty was that library: a library that doesn't bother with cards, because everyone knows everyone's name. Lost in the flash flood were nearly five thousand books, or eighty percent of the collection. Gone was the entire children's section—every book that wasn't checked out. Gone were first editions by Vermont writers Rowland Robinson and Dorothy Canfield Fisher.

And gone was the library itself, the room by the river that had housed all those books for the last sixty-five years. The building was still standing once the water had receded, but the librarian, Linda Norton, vowed that she would never put books back in the room on the banks of the river.

The morning after the flood, when the rain had finally stopped and the New Haven River had fallen back behind its banks, a good part of Lincoln gathered at the library to begin sorting through the mess. As I watched my neighbors work, I was reminded of Bradstreet's loss and what her neighbors must have found and felt the next day.

Certainly, none of my friends had ever seen so many ruined books, and they were stunned. They moved inside the library with robotic deliberation, lifting from the floor the card catalogs, which had been spilled by the waters like ransacked dresser drawers, and tossing the books—saturated with river water and coated with mud—into blue recycling tubs.

Among the people who had come to clean up the mess and salvage whatever they could were teenagers and elementary school students, as well as senior citizens in their seventies and eighties. Many of them worked there all of Saturday, and then came back for more on Sunday.

It has been almost four months since that flood, and still I'm not sure which was more wrenching: the morning after the library was swamped, when my neighbors and I could see and touch the thousands of books that were destroyed, or the odd hollow that we endured in July, when the reality of a life without a library hit home.

Though Norton reopened a minimalist interpretation of her once splendid collection in the upstairs of the town hall in the middle of August—and though the community has embarked upon a capital campaign to replace the books that were ruined and to construct a new building in a new location—all of us in Lincoln learned this summer exactly what it meant to live in a village without a library.

We all understand on some level that there is something sacred about a book. Few people, after all, collect first editions of videocassettes or look for signed copies of CDs. So a roomful of books—especially a roomful of shared books, of books that have been savored and read and literally touched by one's neighbors—is particularly magical.

Lincoln has had a public library for ninety-nine years.

Although a century isn't an especially long history for a library—the oldest continuous lending library in Vermont, the Brookfield Free Library, has been around since 1791—it isn't shabby.

Since the early 1930s, the library had been housed in Burnham Hall, a brick mesa of a building in the center of the village. Burnham's top floor was used for activities and town functions—everything from African dancing on Tuesday nights to the town's annual meeting each March—while the basement housed a dining room, a kitchen, and the library.

The basement library wasn't large: a mere five hundred square feet, plus a small storeroom in the back. It was never the sort of library where scholars would research Daniel Shays's insurrection or scan months of newspaper microfiche to understand the Vietnam War. The fact is there was no microfiche. The periodical room consisted of a card table with magazines, most of them donated: dog-eared *Smithsonians,* well-thumbed *National Geographics.*

But it was always inviting and cozy, and somehow Norton had managed to squeeze six thousand books into the space by the time the New Haven River filled it with five feet of water. Six thousand is not a huge number—eight times that many books were damaged at the Boston Public Library in August when a water main ruptured—but it's impressive for rural Vermont. Moreover, those six thousand books were choice.

On any given day, Norton was as likely to display a new novel by the archly comic British writer Martin Amis as she was a new biography of the Vermont-born president, Calvin Coolidge. Though she was always careful to purchase a variety of mysteries and bestsellers—the staples of any library—she also acquired literary novels, picture books, and esoteric explorations of nature.

One day last spring when I was writing about dandelions, I

wandered by her library to see what she had on the wildflower. I walked home with thirteen books.

Before the flood, the library was open three days a week: Monday, Wednesday, and Saturday. In addition, every Friday morning the library held a story hour for preschoolers and their parents.

Though the room's ambience was created largely by the novels and histories in their clear plastic coats, it was never a mere roomful of books. It was a gathering place. I don't recall ever visiting there and being alone. In the afternoon, I could count on finding any number of senior citizens—eighty-three-year-old Margaret Harris, perhaps, or sixty-six-year-old Darlene Simmons. In the evenings, there were likely to be younger adults and parents with their junior high school–aged teenagers—though Wednesday nights could also be a wonderful wild card.

Nancy MacDonald has been volunteering on Wednesdays at the library for two decades, beginning the year she was pregnant with her oldest daughter. One autumn Wednesday a few years ago, Robert Hicks and Reed Prescott III appeared about the same time. Hicks crafts harpsichords for a living, and Prescott is a painter. Hicks happened to have a harpsichord in his car, and he brought it inside and started to play. Prescott returned home for the painting he was working on, and he brought it back for MacDonald's and Hicks's opinions.

It was, MacDonald recalls, like a little salon.

With the library closed for most of the summer, MacDonald was lost on Wednesday nights. The first evening she would normally have been there, she turned to her husband and confessed that she felt like a ship without a harbor.

Libraries in many small towns are like that. They're community centers. It doesn't matter if they have carefully planned programs for adults—world travelers with their slides from Nepal, chefs with their recipes for ginger pumpkin mousse—or well-orchestrated story hours for toddlers. It doesn't matter if they offer adult literacy programs or seminars on estate planning. They're still magnets for human contact. That's probably why they continue to matter even now, in an era when so much research can be done electronically on the Internet, and books can be found online.

MacDonald wasn't the only Lincoln resident who felt a little unhinged when the library was washed away. Most of us did. Elizabeth Saslaw had to find new excursions for her five-year-old daughter, Bridgette. Marjorie Bernoudy, who had only moved to Lincoln in March, had lost what she considered her base—the place where she was meeting her neighbors and getting to know them.

Some borrowers, of course, began using libraries in neighboring towns, which graciously offered free library cards. Others bought more books than usual. And some simply reread books in their private collections.

But it wasn't the same. A library, regardless of its size, is a social center, and Norton never shushed a soul in three decades as librarian.

Not long after the flood, I went to a library in a nearby town. It was a Wednesday, and none of the faces I had come to associate with my library that day were there. I didn't recognize a soul. It's odd, but other people's libraries can be intimidating, while yours can be your very best friend. That's one of the things that makes a community's public library very special. Moreover, the faces you see at a library are young and old and determinedly middle-aged. By their very nature, libraries are generationally democratic. They cater to everyone. School and work or classes and clubs may separate us, segregating us by interest and age. But libraries remain one of the few places in this world that still bring us together.

The Lincoln Library reopened in temporary quarters on August 12 with about two thousand books: perhaps twelve hundred that survived the flood, and another eight hundred new (or almost new) ones that were donated in July. The week the library opened, the shelves marked "Juvenile Nonfiction" were completely empty, and the adult fiction section skewed heavily to the A's and B's, the books that had been on the very top shelves the night of the flood.

Norton estimates there are at least another two thousand used books that were donated that haven't been filed yet. Her guess is that perhaps a fifth of them will become a part of the permanent collection, and the rest will be sold to raise money for new books and a new building.

The Lincoln Library has never had its own building, and Norton believes that it is now time. Until then, the library will remain upstairs in Burnham Hall's large common room. And though it will take hundreds of thousands of dollars to construct a new library and restock the collection, my sense is that within two or three years the town will have both. Lincoln isn't a rich community, but it knows what it wants. We elect three selectmen to run our town, for instance, but five trustees to manage our library.

Moreover, on the morning after the waters had drenched much of the library and the town gathered to try to save what remained, I saw dazed adults crying softly as they worked. They didn't cry that day for the roads or the bridges that had been lost, they didn't cry for the Burnham Hall kitchen that was destroyed alongside the library. But they did cry for their books—just as I believe that Anne Bradstreet and her neighbors mourned theirs.

WALK THE POSTAL ROUTE WITH A MAILMAN TO GET TO KNOW THE TOWN

TEN SUMMERS AGO, I heard that an acquaintance from college I hadn't seen in eight years was attending the Bread Loaf School of English in Ripton and house-sitting somewhere in Bristol.

I thought it would be nice to catch up, and I sent him a letter with his name and the most precise address I could come up with:

ASPIRING WRITER
HOUSE-SITTING SOMEWHERE
BRISTOL, VT 05443

He received the letter the very next day, and for the last decade I have marveled at the mysterious power of the U.S. Postal Service's Bristol branch.

No more. The Bristol post office's secret is out, and it's a guy named Ron: Ron Williamson, to be precise.

Williamson is a mailman, and when he retires December 29, he will have been a letter carrier for thirty-four years and nine days. He might have been one even longer, but he taught school for ten years before deciding as a young man with a family that it made financial sense for his part-time job with the U.S. Postal Service to become his full-time one.

He is sixty-four, and he still walks eight miles a day around Bristol—the great loping strides of a man in excellent physical condition—with a mailbag slung over his shoulder that often holds thirty to thirty-five pounds of mail. He performs his foot route in the middle of the day, after sorting mail in the early morning and before delivering yet more mail by truck in the afternoon.

Last week I took a walk around Bristol with Williamson, and though I didn't need oxygen or cardiopulmonary resuscitation, I was tired . . . and mightily impressed.

Yet it wasn't simply Williamson's physical stamina that earned my admiration, nor was it his ability to sense black ice with preternatural skill. It wasn't even his cheerful indifference to the cold: Although the temperature didn't top eighteen degrees the day we marched around the village together, he didn't wear a glove on his right hand. A glove, he explained, makes it difficult to separate the mail at each stop.

Rather, it was the way the man serves day in and day out as one of those unobserved but vital buttresses that support a neighborhood, and, in fact, gives the word *neighbor* its profound resonance.

At some houses on our walk, we do not place the mail in the postbox, but we leave it inside the front porch so a senior citizen doesn't have to navigate the icy steps. At others, we deliver stamps (as well as mail) for the shut-ins who don't get out as much as they'd like, and we stay and chat for a few minutes because this visit might be all the company they will have for the day.

Williamson can rifle off the names of the families (and their dogs) on each and every street in the village, tell you who is home and away and (yes) the names of the house-sitters. He can tell you the history of each home.

There is the house in which Leena Ladeau lived. When she was alive, he couldn't pass by without stopping for freshly baked cookies or hot coffee.

Here is Sam McKinnon's house, and no one, it seems, has a better memory for Bristol minutiae than Sam, despite the fact he is flirting with the age of ninety-two.

Mail is magic. Even now, an era in which e-mail governs so much of our business communication and the telephone is our constant companion, the arrival of our mail six days a week retains the ability to excite us. There are a variety of reasons for this, not the least of which, I imagine, are the handcrafted nature of the personal letter and the reality that all mail allows for a critical third dimension—bulk, if you will, and I use that word advisedly—that neither e-mail nor the telephone offers.

But there is another reason that sometimes transcends the content: the delivery itself, and the way people like Williamson link us with our neighbors and remind us why we live where we do.

IT'S THE CREAM CHEESE BROWNIES
THAT BRING OUT THE VOTE

THE OTHER DAY I told my father in Fort Lauderdale how one votes here in Lincoln. We were discussing our process because South Florida is clearly no more capable of handling a modern election than it is a blizzard in April. This is the corner of the country, after all, that in 2000 brought us the terms "hanging chad" and "pregnant chad" (an oxymoron if ever there was one), and in 2002 introduced computer voting machines that would have befuddled the engineers behind the Nintendo GameCube.

I told my father that our procedure is pretty straightforward. On election morning I walk from my house to the dining room in Burnham Hall, the closest thing we have here in Lincoln to a town hall. We vote in the dining room for a lot of reasons, but I believe the most important is that invariably there is a bake sale sponsored by the Ladies' Auxiliary of the Lincoln Volunteer Fire Company and it seems appropriate to have the sale in close proximity to the hall's kitchen.

I don't honestly know whether more people vote because they can purchase homemade apple pie at a price so agreeable it is almost embarrassing, or whether the Ladies' Auxiliary chooses this moment to have a bake sale because there is already so much traffic at the hall. This is one of those great chicken-and-egg questions, though I will confess that I once voted in a mean-ingless primary because I heard there were some delicious angioplasty-causing cream cheese brownies for sale.

When I arrive, Eleanor Scully crosses my name off the town list. You can vote early here in Lincoln, but you can't vote often. Eleanor, who happens to be a member of the local rescue squad, helps out with elections while her husband, Bud—who hasn't let a little thing like lung cancer interfere with his own responsibili-ties on the rescue squad—handles her shift at the rescue station.

Mary Pierce, the organist at the local church, hands me a bal-lot, a piece of paper about twice the size of a diner place mat. The document has thick black boxes separating each office, and the name of each candidate in type about the same size as the print in a Curious George picture book. It's nice and big.

I take my ballot into a wooden kiosk with a curtain that shields me from the waist up, and there I use a pencil to make my choices. The ballot instructs me to make an "X" in the boxes beside the names of the candidates for whom I would like to vote, and informs me precisely how many candidates to vote for in each section: two state senators, for example, or seven justices of the peace. There are lines on which I may write in a name, if I am feeling either curmudgeonly or rebellious.

When I exit the kiosk there is a ballot box waiting. It has a thin slot at the top, so my privacy is preserved—though I know if I were one the folks who stands vigil beside it, once in a while I'd peek.

After the polls close, our town clerk, Kathy Mikkelsen, rounds up her volunteers to count the ballots. We don't have spe-cial auditors like the Academy Awards, but we have representa-tives from the mighty impressive-sounding Board of Civil Authority, and that has always been good enough for me.

The next day I wander by the general store, and Vaneasa Stearns, the owner, informs me who won.

That's all there is to it, and even separated by 1,600 miles I could tell that my father was shaking his head the way he does whenever he learns that another Belgium-sized tract of land in the Everglades is about to be turned into condominiums. To paraphrase Elvis Costello, my father used to be disgusted. Now he tries to be amused.

Unfortunately, Florida will never be able to vote the way we do here in Lincoln—the way we do in most of Vermont. It's too crowded. It's too impersonal. And those cream cheese brownies wouldn't stand a chance in the South Florida heat.

THE SLOWEST DRIVER IN VERMONT

I NOTICED THE flashing lights behind me just north of a freshly cut field of corn, and pulled over beside a ramshackle white equipment barn.

The state trooper, a woman about my age, asked me if I knew I was driving seventy-five miles per hour in a fifty-mile zone.

I told her that I did, and explained, "I had to go that fast. I was passing a truck going sixty."

This was the wrong answer. As a result of that truck, that trooper, and that ticket (my second), I now have nine points on my driver's license—or one short of hitchhiking.

By necessity I have become, I am confident, the slowest driver in Vermont: slower than my neighbor Ray Grimes, who was ninety-two this winter (only a few years older than his rust-red pickup truck); and slower even than the long yellow school bus that honked at me to speed up just south of Starksboro one morning at 7:15.

Now I'm not proud of being the slowest driver in Vermont. It is a distinction without glory, a notoriety born of the aggravation I inflict on all who must drive behind me. Though perhaps not literally cruel and unusual punishment, the time I spend with this scarlet "A" (Acceleration) upon my license is proving to be a sentence of far more consequence than the simple monetary fines I paid for my transgressions.

Burlington, for instance, is thirty-two miles from my home here in Lincoln. I must now drive each and every one of those miles at exactly five miles below the speed limit. Forty-five miles per hour in a fifty-mile zone, twenty-five miles per hour in the thirty-mile zones. I can no longer pass the dump trucks that emerge like dinosaurs from the Hinesburg gravel pits and lumber north toward Burlington at thirty miles an hour. I can no longer race through the yellow traffic lights in Williston, but instead must coast to a stop before them and wave politely at whoever has stopped behind me and honked.

And although most of those thirty-two miles are on Vermont's Route 116, an extremely scenic little road dotted with dairy farms and villages, how many trips will it take before the wonder of the largest manure storage tank in the county wears thin?

I estimate that my new pace has added somewhere between ten and fifteen minutes each way to the drive.

Time, however (or lost time, more exactly), is the least horrific part of being the slowest driver in Vermont. There is an element to my punishment that is far worse.

I have become an automotive pariah, a thing to be avoided, a car to be shunned by my peers on the road. I know this because

I have seen it in the eyes and scowls of my fellow drivers as they pass by me, often glancing to their sides to view the source of their frustration.

Certainly some drivers find me more aggravating than others, but it has now gotten to the point where I can tell almost instantly the degree of contempt I will see abruptly beside me by the way a driver warms up to pass.

There are, essentially, two kinds of tailgaters. There are the passive-aggressors, and then there are the aggressive-passers. No small distinction, this.

The passive-aggressors are those drivers who pull up directly behind me, but are—for whatever the reason—afraid to pass. Passive-aggressors tend to be hunched forward over their steering wheels, and often look as if they are trying to blow my car forward with their exasperated breaths. They believe that by driving as close as possible to my rear bumper, they can literally will me to drive faster. (Uh-uh. With nine points, not a chance.) Eventually they become desperate enough to pass, glaring at me as they whiz by with a look that would wither fruit.

The aggressive-passers, on the other hand, usually appear out of nowhere. One moment there is nothing in my rearview mirror, and the next there is a monster pickup truck with tires as big as a house. And then—just as suddenly—it is pulling into the passing lane, it is beside me, and then it is gone. Aggressive-passers don't scowl at me the way the passive-aggressors do. Occasionally they will glance at me, register brief surprise at the fact that I'm nowhere near ninety years old, and shake their heads. But usually they just fly by.

I tend to believe that the passive-aggressors hate me more than the aggressive-passers because they spend more time behind me. They stew.

Now I don't think any of this would bother me quite so much if I could just explain to these people that I did not become the slowest driver in Vermont by choice, that I drive the way I do because I have to. One of these days I just may take my wife up on her suggestion to have a bumper sticker printed that reads, "Have mercy on me. I'm a nine-pointer."

VERMONT HAS CHANGED—BUT NOT ITS PEOPLE

SIXTY YEARS AGO this month, Marjorie Vosburgh took a ride on one of the family workhorses in the high hills between Lincoln and Ripton. The ride lasted barely four hours and covered no more than a couple of miles, but it's an interesting barometer both of how much Vermont has been transformed in the past six decades and yet how little its people—when they are at their best—have changed.

It was February 1943, and Vosburgh was fourteen. She lived with her family on what was then a common-sized dairy farm—twenty cows and a couple of horses—three miles south of Lincoln village. Their farm sat at the intersection of the roads that led west into Bristol Notch and south into Ripton, at an elevation of roughly 1,800 feet. In a winter snowstorm, they were the very end of the line, even for the postman, who most days was a study in fortitude and perseverance.

On this particular day, however, the postman could drive no farther than her family's farm. The storm was one massive white-out, and the snow was piling high on the roads back to Bristol. And so he delivered her family's mail, and left them as well with the correspondence for the farms farther down the road. Perhaps those other families could pick it up from them over the next couple of days.

Among the letters Vosburgh spied was one from Sgt. Ralph Hamilton, addressed to his parents, Mr. and Mrs. Walter Hamilton. The younger Hamilton had enlisted soon after the United States had entered World War II and was stationed in the South Pacific. Vosburgh knew that his parents hadn't heard from the soldier in weeks and had grown worried.

There were no phones and no electricity yet in this corner of Addison County, so Vosburgh couldn't simply pick up the telephone and call the Hamiltons with the news that a letter had arrived from their son. Nor could she ask one of her parents to drive the few miles south to the Hamilton farm, not with the roads buried under snow.

And so she did the only thing she could. She put a bridle on Queenie, one of the dappled gray workhorses her father used on the farm, and started off in the storm to the Hamiltons' house.

The ride was an adventure for Vosburgh. First of all, Queenie was a workhorse, not a saddle horse. Her family didn't even own a saddle, so Vosburgh was riding the animal bareback, clinging to the animal's mane and bridle as she tried to navigate the tempest.

Second, the snow beyond their house was almost up to the horse's belly. Once Vosburgh slipped underneath Queenie. At another point, she simply had to climb off the animal and lead her through a patch of waist-deep snow.

But she made it to the Hamilton family's farm, where Ralph's mother greeted her at the front door. Though the woman later admitted that she wondered what Vosburgh was doing on her front stoop covered in snow in the midst of a blizzard, she said simply, "Well, look who's here."

Sixty years later, Vosburgh says she won't forget the rapturous gaze—part wonder, part relief—that filled Mrs. Hamilton's face when she told her that she'd brought a letter from her son.

"Seeing that smile was worth anything I went through," she recalls now at seventy-four.

Nevertheless, it is hard for her to fathom that a mere six decades ago so many Vermonters lived without electricity or phone lines or even running water. But live they did.

Ralph Hamilton died last month in Ohio, though his sister, Lida Hamilton Cloe, eighty-seven, remains here in Lincoln. She is among the neighbors who are helping Vosburgh these days endure a bad patch with her back and her hip.

"I look out for Marjorie," Cloe says. "She's a very good friend of mine."

Many of the outward trappings of our world indeed have been revolutionized by technology, but the basic generosity that marked Vermont sixty years ago remains unchanged.

LIFE, LIBERTY, AND PLENTY
OF CHARMIN

TOMORROW MORNING, I will join my neighbors from Bristol, Starksboro, and Lincoln and celebrate the birth of our nation, that day in 1776 when a small group of patriots in Philadelphia put their pens to paper and their necks on the line, and declared that their outhouses would no longer be subject to English tyranny.

As many historians have noted, the Revolutionary War was the last great armed conflict fought over outhouses. It was Thomas Paine himself who wrote that fateful summer of '76, "Tyranny is the hell that sits on the throne—far from the paper."

Even Ethan Allen, an otherwise tireless self-promoter, admits in his account of the capture of Fort Ticonderoga that the British would never have surrendered and come out if they'd had an outhouse inside the fort's walls.

In any case, of all the towns in Vermont that accord Independence Day the respect it deserves, it is Bristol alone that understands the crucial role the outhouse played convincing Thomas Jefferson to get off the pot and draft the Declaration of Independence. As it has every Fourth of July for a decade and a half now, Bristol will celebrate the bombs bursting in air with a series of outhouse races, beginning tomorrow morning at 8:30.

Conceived, managed, and run by the Bristol Rotary Club, the outhouse races are a combination of the great chariot races from *Ben-Hur* and the low-tech wizardry of a Pinewood Derby.

The outhouses that race are powered by people, and the rules are fairly specific:

- As many as four people may pull or push the contraption, but there must be one person sitting inside it in a position that reflects what those in the outhouse race world might describe as anatomic and functional accuracy.

- The outhouse must resemble, as this year's organizer Ted Lylis puts it, "an old-fashioned one-holer." The sides must be covered, the wheels must be rotating casters, and—for reasons I hate to imagine—the floor must be solid.

The current outhouse race course is a straight path down Bristol's Main Street, with the village's lone stoplight as its finish line. In past years, however, the course has actually wound its way around the Bristol commons, which meant there were the sort of sharp curves that occasionally resulted in accidents between outhouses (versus accidents *in* outhouses, which is a whole other premise I'm not going to touch).

It's not surprising that the idea of an outhouse race was conceived at the sort of New Year's Eve party in which there was rigorous intellectual debate. In the midst of one especially animated discussion of philosopher John Locke's influence on Jefferson, Rotarian Larry Gile turned to Rotarian Bill Paine, or Paine to Gile (no one's quite sure who's to blame), and said, "Hey, let's have an outhouse race."

And while I've no doubt that the outhouse races are a fascinating historical re-creation of the Revolutionary War charges and countercharges that occurred on Vermont soil at the breakfast battle of Hubbardton, their real role today is as Rotary fund-raisers.

Through a combination of race entry fees and spectator wagers, the outhouse races some years raise a sizable sum of money for the Rotary Club to return to the community. This spring, for example, the Bristol Rotary awarded four $500 scholarships to high school seniors. Much of that money was raised from last year's outhouse race.

And so tomorrow, in addition to savoring the parades and fireworks and barbecues that commemorate the great spirit of '76, I will also watch that unique homage to the outhouse's place in colonial history. I will take the time to pay my respects to the thunderbox, to cheer on the Revolutionary War's armored personnel carriers and commodes, and salute those women and men who remember the courage of Hancock and Hale by racing one-holers.

MEETINGS MESSY BY NECESSITY

WHENEVER I WORRY that town meetings are going the way of the dinosaur and thumbing a ride to extinction, I talk to my neighbor Dave Marsters. Marsters has been moderating town meetings in Lincoln for twelve years, standing serenely at the front of Burnham Hall before the long rows of folding chairs still made of wood.

Once again Monday night he will be on stage—literally, as well as figuratively—protected from the chaos he calls neighbors the other 364 days of the year by a slim book called *Robert's Rules of Order.*

Marsters, more than anyone else, is capable of reassuring me that the town meeting is not quite ready for the respirator. "Attendance goes up and down," he says thoughtfully, "but I haven't seen a pattern of diminishing attendance over the last decade."

A decade is roughly how long I've been going to town meeting. I went to my first one in 1987 and have since learned the three basic rules:

- When the moderator requests that you keep your comments "germane," it means it's time to sit down. You've lost all touch with the discussion at hand, and what you think sounds to your neighbors like the Gettysburg Address is in reality a big bowl of meandering word goop.

- "Graders" and "grader chains" have something to do with the town assets and the town budget—not the school assets and the school budget. "Grader" questions, therefore, should be directed to the Board of Selectmen.

- Never propose an amendment to an amendment, unless the article involves a budget appropriation in the upper six figures, and you want to make sure the debate goes on into April . . . or you want simply to fluster the moderator.

Marsters loves town meeting, especially when the discussions grow animated. His biggest fear? We're growing too civil as a culture.

"I'm really scared when people tell me, 'I shouldn't say that in town meeting.' The fact is, if you feel that strongly about it, you should say it," Marsters insists. "Think back on the things people used to say. People really did debate things, and things really did get hot—and it wasn't just because of the old stove that used to sit in the center of the town hall."

One of Marsters's favorite memories is the town meeting four years ago when it looked like the Lincoln school budget might fail—a first for the town. The irony of that memory is that Dave Marsters, private citizen, father and teacher, wanted desperately to see the budget pass.

He recalls how "the debate was long and detailed, exactly what it needed to be. People finally agreed that we absolutely couldn't afford the budget as a town, yet that didn't matter: It was important for the kids that we pass it. And what was really meaningful was that people left the hall feeling that they'd had the opportunity to speak their voice."

Marsters wonders if the biggest threat to town meetings isn't one of the usual suspects we round up this time of the year: suburban sprawl and the demise of the village; the end of the volunteer ethic; the time pressures put upon the two-career couple.

Marsters fears a more insidious drift. "There is a cultural trend in our society to make democracy quick and easy, just like everything else. And that eliminates the hard work that real democracy demands," he says. He cites the initiatives that appear every year to replace public voice votes with Australian, or all-day secret, balloting. The result, he says, "is a lot more people voting who haven't been a part of the discussion."

Marsters's moral? He has two. Democracy takes time; at the very least, a single Monday night or one Tuesday a year. And, at its best, it will be a messy business.

Perhaps that's why someone long ago picked the first week in March for Town Meeting Day: What better way is there to emerge from a winter's hibernation than to gather as a tribe in the center of town and welcome in mud season with the sloppy but satisfying work of self-governance?

VILLAGE'S CENTER STARTS IN AISLE ONE

DESPITE MY DEEP appreciation for electronic mail and the power of the Internet to ferret out information quickly, we have yet to invent a means of communication as efficient, speedy, or dependable as a good general store.

We have that sort of emporium in Lincoln: well-stocked aisles of bread and canned goods, a couple of refrigerator cases and freezers, and a small hardware section in the back, all serving as the front, essentially, for the sort of impressively low-tech transmission station or relay center that must make phone companies jealous.

Everyone in Lincoln, of course, understands this. If you absolutely must get a message to somebody fast . . . you call the store. If you simply must know why the fire engines just left the station . . . you phone the store. If you have to leave town in a hurry and need someone to milk your three-hundred-pound llama . . . well, you call the store.

Husband and wife co-owners Dan and Vaneasa Stearns have become human fiber-optic cables, linking the village in ways no technology ever could.

One day this summer, I saw how we depend upon them. I was in the midst of the sort of home repairs that demand an hour from most guys and take me about a week. So I wound up walking to the store every few minutes in need of yet another three-cent nut or four-cent bolt, or some free (but invaluable) advice from Dan about how to drill a new screw hole into a metal light fixture.

In the time it took me to visit the store three times, Vaneasa received four phone calls.

Nancy Stevens, the local private investigator (every village needs one) and llama-meister, had to travel abruptly to Boston, leaving behind Holly, her llama, and Holly's new calf, Barn Baby. Barn Baby was going through a phase in which she insisted on nursing from a barn beam instead of from Holly (hence the name), and so Nancy needed someone to help her friend Ruth Shepherd milk Holly until she returned and could get Barn Baby back on llama-manna instead of pumpkin pine.

And since you won't find an assistant llama-milker in the Yellow Pages and Nancy needed one fast . . . she called Vaneasa.

A problem? Nope. Vaneasa instantly thought of Pam Smith, because Pam keeps a thousand-pound Scottish Highlander Hereford Cross beef cow as a pet and probably wouldn't mind holding Holly while Ruth was working the business end of a particularly woolly milk machine.

A few moments later, local septic-system cleaner Alan Clark needed to reach local excavator Chris Acker right away, so he called Vaneasa and asked her to have Chris call him. Now, when you're a septic-system cleaner and you need an excavator, you don't mess around. Time is, well, of the essence.

And so Clark didn't waste precious minutes leaving a message at Acker's company and he certainly couldn't count on a cellular phone in Lincoln. As Priscilla Presley and a forty-person film crew discovered two years ago, cell phones don't work in our hills.

Did Acker get Clark's message quickly? You bet. Acker arrived at the store in search of a ham salad sandwich less than ten minutes after the local septic-tank czar had left a bulletin for him there.

Yet the flurry of phone calls was not yet complete. Vaneasa would receive two more that would have nothing to do with such inventory staples as Slim Jims and Pepsi and crawlers.

First, she was called by an out-of-state real estate agent she'd never met who wanted to know what properties might be for rent this winter in Lincoln. And then a Middlebury resident called in search of our town clerk, after mistaking the unique whistle and ding the phone makes in our town office for evidence the phone was out of order.

Can you count on the Internet this way? Did we ever get this kind of mother's milk from Ma Bell? Not a chance.

Nope, if you really want to reach out and touch someone, you're better off just calling the store.

THE SCHOOL—
PLAYGROUNDS AND
CLASSROOMS

DRAMA LIVES IN PRESCHOOL
OZ ODYSSEY

NEITHER BETHANY BARNER nor Victoria Brown is the sort of actress who enjoys discussing her craft. But as they await the curtain for the first performance of their new show, the dramatic difference in their approaches becomes clear.

Four-year-old Victoria is a study in silent concentration. In the last seconds before she will walk onto the redwood deck that today is a stage, the only time she moves is when she methodically checks her props one last time.

Wicker basket? Got it. Red sneakers that will serve today as my ruby slippers? Yup, still on my feet. Those ribbons that Mom put in my pigtails? Phew, still there.

Five-year-old Bethany, on the other hand, is already deeply immersed in her role. She has become one with the little dog she will bring to life. She falls to her hands and knees and barks with great enthusiasm.

"That's what I'm going to say to the Wicked Witch," she explains to the audience members as they take their seats on blankets in the grass.

Certainly there are drama critics who fear for the future of the living theater, but I'm not among them.

After all, I'm not a drama critic.

Nevertheless, these days I still find myself waxing poetic and growing downright ebullient when I contemplate the future of the live stage play. Recently I saw that future in the form of the Lincoln Cooperative Preschool's performance of *The Wizard of Oz*, and I was reassured that today's young crop of actors and actresses brings a passion to their craft that will keep the theater vibrant and alive for a long time.

Among the new faces to look for at, perhaps, the Royall Tyler Theatre in the year 2010:

First there is five-year-old Steven Patterson. With tremendous sensitivity, Steven brought the deeply conflicted Scarecrow to life, especially in those moments when he was suddenly surrounded by five of the seven little girls who thought it was their turn to be Dorothy.

Likewise, Bridgette Bartlett, four, demonstrated the sort of honesty in her performance in which the fine line between the world and the stage all but disappears. "I think I want to give my mommy a kiss," she said soon after meeting the Tin Man, at which point she simply walked off the stage and into her mother's lap and did just that.

Three-year-old Cameron Skerritt Perta brought immense energy to the role of Flying Monkey (on and off the stage), and Alexandra Ackert-Smith (still a few weeks short of three), conveyed with elegance the despair of the witch as she melted.

Ackert-Smith also made an excellent scary face on command.

Viscaya Du Mond Wagner and Emily Wood were both equally reassuring good witches from the north, and worked well as a tag-team sort of Glinda.

Of course, the performance needed multiple Glindas because there were so many different Dorothys. At one point, Viscaya and Emily were outnumbered four to two, and the witches had to work pretty darn fast to get all four girls back to Kansas.

As an added bonus, the show was preceded by a rousing rendition of "I Am a Pizza" in both English and French, an appropriate opening number given the pizza's wistful, Dorothy-like plea at the end of the song: "I am a pizza, please take me home."

Directed by outgoing preschool teacher Nancy Stevens, this version of *Oz* was particularly rich in improvisational flair. Sometimes a good witch just needs her mom, and that's A-OK, and sometimes the Munchkins will be more difficult to herd than a litter of kittens.

And that's OK, too. Because Oz is a pretty magical place to begin with, and it can only become more enchanting when peopled by actors little more than three feet tall.

IT'S NOT EASY TO BE A KID

LAST MONTH I had the pleasure of serving as the company for an "unaccompanied minor" on a flight from Portland, Oregon, to Chicago. The minor was a ten-year-old boy on his way to catch up with his mom in Florida during his spring break from school, and we became pals soon after the flight attendant—a woman who had had her smile surgically removed at birth—pointed out his seat to him and commanded, "Read the safety card before we take off."

We bonded because I was willing to explain to him why Billy Bob Thornton was trying to blackmail Frances McDormand's boss in *The Man Who Wasn't There,* and he was willing to teach me how to draw the Pokémon character Pikachu.

At first he had been mildly annoyed that the flight was showing a movie for grown-ups instead of one for children, but when

I pointed out to him that he was the only child on the entire airplane, he saw the reasonableness of the airline's decision to show a black-and-white Coen brothers film over *Jimmy Neutron.*

Personally, I would have been content to watch *Jimmy Neutron,* too, but then I will watch anything while inside an airplane. I'd watch a two-hour infomercial about nose hair trimmers if it took my mind off the fact that I was hurtling through space at 500 mph, and there was nothing between me and the earth but 35,000 feet of air.

In any case, I liked this young man a lot, especially because he understood the cardinal rules of flying in the modern age: Wear sneakers and travel with lots of snacks. In his knapsack he had pretzels covered in chocolate and pretzels covered in yogurt, Tootsie Rolls, Chex Party Mix, juice boxes, and three Twinkies. He was also willing to share his cache with me, even though I could offer nothing in return but a couple of Altoids and the antibacterial hand gel with which we could wash our hands when we were done.

Incidentally, the sneakers matter because there seems to be a dramatically decreased likelihood that you will have to take your shoes off at security if you are wearing a pair of Converse low-tops (my traveling sneaker of choice) than if you are wearing black leather wing tips. There is nothing worse than being caught with your shoes off when it is announced that your flight has been canceled and you need to return to the counter to book a new one.

The boy had spiked his hair with gobs of gel so that it looked like Needles National Park, and he had brought with him a series of toy skateboards the size of disposable razors. We spent a few minutes on the flight rolling the skateboards back and forth on his tray table and he showed me how to make them flip. This gave us both enormous satisfaction because the gentleman in the seat before him had insisted on putting his seat back so that the headrest was practically in the boy's lap, and every time we flipped a skateboard we jostled the guy's seat. (We had politely asked this fellow to put his seat forward, but he said he liked to recline and suggested that the boy move to any of the empty seats on the plane if it disturbed him to have a view of a strange man's balding scalp.)

In Chicago I changed planes, but the boy was going to remain on board because the flight continued on to Tampa, his eventual destination. When we were parting I wished him well and he said—seemingly out of the blue—that he hadn't seen his real father in almost two years.

I nodded and wondered suddenly who had put him on the plane in Portland. Then I gave him my card.

Sometimes, it's very hard to be a kid.

THE THRILL, THE STRESS, THE JOY OF THE RACE

IN A SHORT RACE, a thousandth of a second can make all the difference: the difference between a fleeting but precious moment inside the winner's circle, and a lifetime outside it, wondering . . . What if?

And so, despite the fact that his first race is only minutes away, Steve Schubart decides his vehicle needs more weight. With a borrowed steel washer, Scotch tape, and a little faith, he and his race-day mechanic bring the car up to 140.7 grams—still a legal machine, but a weighty one.

I ask him if the track looks fast this brisk March afternoon, but Schubart's a veteran. "It's the car that counts," he says simply.

A moment later, Schubart and his machine—a worker bee of a race car, an earth-tone, pine-colored rocket with more heart than hieroglyphics—are behind the starting peg.

And then the races begin. In a series of head-to-head contests, Schubart's car sizzles down the short course, dueling racers known throughout the circuit for speed. Guys like Mike Truchon, this year behind a dark red machine with lightning bolts on the hood so vivid you can sense the way the car will explode down the track. Or Brian Mayo, whose silver racer looks so powerful one spectator in the crowd murmurs approvingly, "Give that thing enough fuel and I'll bet it goes into orbit."

Schubart will never know if the washer—a flat piece of metal roughly the size of a city subway token—made the difference. The races were close, two with Mayo so tight that not even the video cameras and stopwatches surrounding the finish line could determine a winner.

But, in the end, Steve Schubart's gritty car squeaked out a few key victories, and he took first place in the Webelo Den, and third place overall in Lincoln Cub Scout Pack 633's Pinewood Derby.

The March 23 race, held in Lincoln's Burnham Hall, is a warm-up of sorts for the Cub Scout District's annual Pinewood Derby in Middlebury on April 27. But just as the Olympic trials for many athletes can mean as much as one moment in time in Athens, Greece, or a year in the minors can mean as much as a week in what's called the Major League Show, last Saturday's Lincoln Derby was an emotional competition.

Sportsmanship always won out over standings, but that doesn't mean the races weren't tense.

The Cub Scouts, all six- to ten-year-olds, had taken identical blocks of nondescript pine and identical plastic wheels, and—perhaps with a little help from Mom or Dad—built their own deeply personal, highly idiosyncratic cars. Of the fifteen racing machines that graced the starting pegs, no two looked as if they were from the same automotive genus or species, or inspired by the same issue of *Cub Scout Car and Driver*. My personal favorite? Six-year-old Bryn Paul made the conscious decision to sacrifice aerodynamics for accuracy, and gave his car a Play-Doh and pipe-cleaner driver.

And each boy brought to the Derby the hope that his car would speed over the thirty-two-foot maple track first and electrify the Burnham Hall crowd. "I love the Derby," says Don Gale, whose son Schuyler is a part of the Pack's Wolf Den. "It's Thunder Road without the noise."

But each also brought a tremendous sense of camaraderie, the sort of friendship in which fairness mattered more than who finally won.

In the Schubart/Mayo face-offs for the Webelo blue ribbon—two so close that a third was needed to determine the winner—it wasn't one of the adult judges who finally awarded the victory to Steve Schubart.

It was Brian Mayo. Even in that third race, Mayo's and Schubart's cars seemed to cross the finish line simultaneously, and the judges were about to insist on a fourth race. But with a voice as filled with enthusiasm as when he'd first entered the hall with his car and his hopes, Mayo called out the words that symbolized the spirit of the Derby:

"Good race! Steve won!"

ISAAC AND GUS SURVIVE GIRL WORLD

ISAAC AND GUS have been to Girl World and back, and don't seem any worse for the wear. Cassidy, too.

And Dillon? Well, Dillon L'Heureux is only three, so he was happy just to be along for the ride.

Isaac Prescott, Gus Yost, and Cassidy Kearns, however, are graybeards at four and five. They've been . . . socialized. They do . . . boy things. Things with trucks. And tractors. A stick is a sword; a fallen branch is a bazooka.

Ah, but there they were at the Lincoln Cooperative Preschool, at the wedding of the dog and the bear—a.k.a. Girl World.

Last month's ceremony was, without question, among the higher peaks of the alpine ridgeline that makes up the frenetic preschool social whirl here in Lincoln. One would never have guessed that it was only the second time that preschool teacher Kerry Malloy had coordinated the nuptials of a pair of stuffed animals. (The first, of course, occurred when Malloy was five.)

It was also a study in just how different boys and girls are. Consider, for a moment, the preparations.

The bride's entourage began arriving at 8:30 in the morning, ninety minutes before the double-ring ceremony. Among the first to arrive was flower girl Bridgette Bartlett, five, wearing a snow-white satin gown with matching shoes. Right behind her was Savannah Mayo, also five, decked out in a hunter-green dress with a scooped neck and poufed ballroom sleeves.

Meanwhile, the groom's pals came in T-shirts and jeans. Briefly Isaac and Dillon had bow ties clipped to their collars, but they didn't last long. As soon as the moms' backs were turned, the bow ties were tossed away like roadkill.

And while the girls immersed themselves in the massive amounts of costume jewelry and bridal accoutrements donated by a local bridal boutique . . . the boys hightailed it to the sand table, where Isaac ran the plow and Gus managed the crane. "We're building a road," Isaac explained earnestly.

The big stuffed dog—the bride—had the ministrations of all the girls in the class. They clipped jewelry to her large, flouncy ears; they placed a veil upon her head. She wore faux pearls and opals and rhinestones. She was offered a gauzy blusher.

But the bear, who was merely the lowly groom, was completely ignored by the boys. Finally, Kerry Malloy used a safety pin to attach a bow tie to his woolly neck.

The two animals were formally wed by Nancy Stevens, a duly elected justice of the peace. There was a brief moment of gender confusion when she took the animals aside for their premarital consultation, since it is usually the men in this world who act like the dogs. But Stevens rallied, and started the service.

First came the bride, escorted by my own four-year-old daughter, Grace (wearing an ankle-length ivory gown, rich with embroidered flowers and lace). Next came the groom, carried by young Cassidy Kearns, four.

Grace carried the bride with the solemnity I'd expect her to show if she'd come across the Holy Grail in the nearby sandpit. Cassidy clutched the groom as if it were a giant, bloodsucking leech he'd found in a swamp.

Now, I don't mean to imply the boys were graceless. Cassidy

certainly rallied, serenading the bride with an a cappella rendition of the Beatles classic "All You Need Is Love," in which he made up for his lack of accompaniment with unfettered enthusiasm.

And, momentarily, the boys and the girls were truly of one mind: When Stevens informed the bear and the dog they could kiss, Grace and Cassidy cautiously brought the stuffed snouts of the two animals together, and then dropped the creatures as if they were radioactive.

Any way you look at it, however, it was a great event. Our planet is, in far too many ways, a man's world. But for one brief and glorious instant this spring, the Lincoln preschoolers were able to glimpse . . . Girl World.

INSPIRING TEACHERS MAKE
EDUCATION WORTH EVERY PENNY

I WAS NEVER scared of the principal when I was in elementary school. The cultural notion that the principal is a disciplinary ogre—an image that has filled children's literature as diverse as Roald Dahl's *Matilda* and a good number of the *Arthur* books by Marc Brown—was not exactly lost on me, but it was always slightly foreign.

The truth is, I don't think any kids at Northeast Elementary School in Stamford, Connecticut, were scared of the principal when I was there in the late 1960s and early 1970s.

I should be precise: Nobody was scared of the assistant principal. There might have been students frightened by the principal, though I'd wager that was largely because he had the intimidating two letters "Dr." before his name.

But the assistant principal—in my memory, at least, a heavyset man with a thick shock of hair that was just starting to gray and the sort of boxy eyeglasses that Hollywood always places on the Mission Control scientists in Gemini- and Apollo-era space movies—was always called Mr. D.

Mr. D. was Joe Dinnan. And Joe Dinnan knew how to talk to children about the things that mattered to them with a knowledge that in hindsight can honestly be considered extraordinary. It was Mr. D. who recommended to me in the school library that I read *Johnny Tremain* in the third grade and then, two years later, remembered my interest in the Revolutionary War and suggested *April Morning*. It was Mr. D. who could mediate a dispute with the potential to grow ugly, a hallway debate in which one group of kids thought Don McLean's "American Pie" was the best song ever written and another contingent was arguing with equal fervor it was the Jackson Five's "I'll Be There."

Mr. D. understood the fact that the New York Mets were in the World Series in 1969 was an event of legitimate historical importance, and we should be witness to it. He allowed my class to watch the game on television—yes, Virginia, once the World Series was actually played in daylight so children could see it, too—even though we were supposed to be learning fractions.

And, what is probably the greatest gift any teacher or administrator can give to a child, he knew how to make us feel special. When, somehow, I would find myself completely alone on the playground during recess or lunch, separate from the running and the goofing and the noise, it was always Mr. D. who would track down a baseball glove, hand me mine, and patiently toss a softball with me until it was time to go in.

Town meeting is fast approaching, and either on Monday night or sometime on Tuesday, many of us will be staring at the rows of numbers that comprise our local school budgets. Sometimes, it's easy to forget that behind all those figures are flesh-and-blood teachers and administrators who, more times than not, are inspiring and impressive and wise.

The principal at the Lincoln elementary school, Bill Jesdale, is a lot like Mr. D. I understand on occasion he is even called Mr. J.

Likewise, I have every faith that the Lincoln teachers my daughter will have—the ones who will teach her to read, the ones who will tell her of Rosa Parks, the ones who will have her watch baby chicks hatch—will be every bit as wondrous as my best memories of the teachers I had when I was a boy. I imagine the same can be said of the teachers in (for example) Richmond, Colchester, or Cornwall.

Consequently, when you look at those charts at town meeting a little later this week, remember that as helpful as those numbers may be, they can never convey how on any given day a good teacher or administrator will make sure a group of small children will know that they matter.

WILL SLEEPING BEAUTY WAKE FOR SCHOOL?

THERE'S A SCHOOL bus stop at the end of my driveway, which for the past two years served as my four-year-old daughter's alarm clock. The Gale and Brown children who would wait there for the bus were the only thing standing between Grace's getting to preschool on time and the inevitable destruction of a million-plus brain cells that would have accompanied her sleeping till 9:00 and then watching the midget Martians who've infiltrated PBS and call themselves Teletubbies.

My daughter would hear the inspiring sounds of the older children waiting for another chance to go to school—a boom box blasting Marilyn Manson, the wheels of in-line skates smashing onto asphalt from the height of the nearby church steeple—and she would peer out her bedroom window with interest.

My wife and I would then be able to cajole her downstairs and get her ready for preschool. The school bus alarm worked wonders because the bus would arrive shortly before 8:00, which meant we had the full hour we needed before preschool began to convince her that Oreos weren't breakfast, and then find an outfit that would appeal to buddies Bridgette and Ellen—a profound enigma, since Ellen wears only overalls and Bridgette wears only skirts.

Now my point isn't that it was difficult to get my daughter out the door—though it could be.

My point is that my daughter sleeps like a mummy. There have been times I've been tempted to put a mirror over her mouth, and mornings when she's slept through the world's most cloying alarm: The Barbie Clock Radio.

"Ding, ding, ding. Hi. I'm Barbie. Ding, ding, ding. Hi. I'm Barbie."

Then it starts emitting the sort of beep that engineers at nuclear power plants hear when a radiation leak has just started twisting carrots into pretzels.

Once, my wife heard the alarm beep eighty-one times before Grace turned it off . . . and then went back to sleep.

Well, tomorrow morning, a few minutes before 8:00, that school bus will once more coast to a stop at the end of our driveway, but for the first time my daughter will be expected to get on it. Tomorrow is her first day of kindergarten, the day she begins going to school.

And so, like many parents, my wife and I have spent weeks wringing our hands at the prospect. We wonder two things:

- How did she grow up so quickly?

- How are we going to convince the neighbor children to start waiting at the bus stop at 7:00 A.M., so we can get Grace out the door by 8:00?

These are universal questions. It really does seem like yesterday that I tried to console my sobbing daughter a few days after she was born by offering her Placebo Breast: I held a pacifier to my naked chest, and told her my chest hair was a sweater. (It worked, but only because Grace was less than a week old and hadn't yet met her fashion-conscious friends Bridgette and Ellen.)

In any case, the first question is easier to answer than the second. Yes, in three months Grace will turn five, but a half-decade isn't really a long time at all. Our president has sex scandals older than that.

The second question poses a real conundrum, however, and my wife and I indeed wonder what we're going to do weekday mornings for the next thirteen years. Our hope—and we cling to it the way I do to every strand of hair on my folliclely challenged cranium—is that by getting her to bed early, she'll wake up early. Perhaps, we delude ourselves, we've simply allowed her to stay up too late all these years, playing and reading and watching Jay Leno. We'll see. We'll certainly know by this time tomorrow whether putting her to bed right after breakfast today did any good. With any luck, she will have gotten on the bus with her lunch box, waved to her parents from the window . . . and not noticed that the two of us were sobbing into our coffee cups.

A CRUSH ON YOUR TEACHER IS
NO EXCUSE TO ACT LIKE A GEEK

WHEN I WAS in fourth grade, I had a crush on my teacher so powerful that during the first days of school the woman must have thought I was mute. I was completely incapable of speaking casually around her, and when she started to call on me in late September, calling on me largely, I imagine, to see what my voice sounded like, my answers were mumbled and soft.

There were many reasons why I had a crush on Thalia Kominos (the name itself was an aphrodisiac). She had a mane of creosote-black hair that cascaded far down her back, a lengthy waterfall indeed because Mrs. Kominos was tall. A statuesque beauty. She was also an immensely gifted teacher, the sort of person who could make even math interesting—no small accomplishment, since I viewed math with the same distaste I had for my mother's cold cabbage and sausage soup.

Moreover, Mrs. Kominos had a teenage daughter roughly my brother's age, and somehow I got the notion into my head— mistaken, I'd learn later—that the girl was dating one of my brother's best friends.

Growing up, there was nothing I wanted more than to be my

popular older brother or one of his friends. He was always class president, he played drums in a garage band that seemed to have weekly gigs at pool parties with gorgeous teen girls, and he achieved straight A's without effort.

Consequently, it was perhaps inevitable that I would become attracted to Thalia Kominos.

In fact, I actually grew protective of her, despite my inability to speak above a whisper around her. When she would lose control of the class, I would actually try to convince my friends to retake their seats or will them to settle down.

It was this protectiveness that caused me to open my mouth that October and say the most embarrassing thing I have ever said in my life.

Mrs. Kominos was trying desperately to keep us interested in the names of the South American capitals. Alas, she was failing: The class was giggling and passing notes, or ignoring her and talking aloud. The room was noisy, a point that matters not simply because it meant that it was difficult to be heard, but because I want to be sure you understand the decibel level of the action that precipitated my small outburst.

Someone (and this is a family newspaper, so I will use the scientific terms) expelled intestinal gas consisting largely of hydrogen, sulfide, and methane. And this person expelled it loudly. It sounded like a rocket ship lifting off.

The result was chaos: The class was howling, groaning, screaming.

It was then that I dramatically altered the trajectory of my year in fourth grade. I slammed my hand down hard on my desk to get the class's attention and said, "Calm down! It's a perfectly natural bodily function."

For a split second the class did grow quiet while they digested my pronouncement, but only for a second. Then the magnitude of what I had just said became clear: I had just called the funniest sound a fourth-grader can make "a perfectly natural bodily function." The class descended into bedlam, and even Mrs. Kominos had to bury her head behind her arms because she was laughing so hard at my colossally geek-like behavior.

It took me months to live that one down, and even by June there was the risk that whatever I said at the playground would elicit the response: "It's a perfectly natural bodily function." I could ask someone the time and he'd look at his watch and answer, "It's a perfectly natural bodily function."

My own daughter will start fourth grade when school begins this Wednesday, and so I have shared this tale with her and with her friends Yuki, Bridgette, and Ellen. I view this as thoughtful parenting.

Good luck, students. Study hard and never (even if you believe you are protecting your teacher) refer to the inadvertent expulsion of intestinal gases as "a perfectly natural bodily function."

DON'T BELIEVE ALL YOU READ: THE KIDS ARE ALL RIGHT

FIVE YEARS AGO my wife and I were watching two young teenage girls in leotards and dance pants, and my wife murmured to me, "Will you look at that posture and poise? That's why you have your daughter take ballet."

Our own daughter was a few weeks shy of four at the time,

and she was one of a dozen preschoolers and kindergartners toddling around in tutus the size of open umbrellas while Jennifer Barden, their dance teacher, worked nobly to keep a straight face, since the first ballet position for most of the kids was toppling over and the second was picking their nose.

The teenagers, Krista Billings and Stephi Needham, were assistant dance teachers, and my wife and I would learn later that they had been dancing with Barden since they were toddlers themselves. Over the last half-decade, my wife and I have seen Billings and Needham as they continued to assist Barden in the dance studio, as well as when they danced themselves in the end-of-the-year recitals.

The two young women did everything from literally holding a child around her waist while she first lifted a leg, ostrich-like, and figured out that she could indeed balance on one foot, to demonstrating how to adjust the laces on a ballet slipper. They knew all their own dances, of course, but also all of the dances that the younger classes would be learning as well.

As a matter of fact, among my very favorite memories of either girl would be the final recital in June 2001, when Needham—then a junior in high school—donned the costume of an apparently very good-natured octopus and danced on the Mount Abraham high school stage with a group of four- and five-year-old pip-squeaks to the old Beatles song "Octopus's Garden." There are not many sixteen-year-old girls in this world who would willingly climb into an octopus costume and dance with kindergartners on a high school stage.

This month Billings and Needham graduated from high school. They will both start college in the fall and will no longer be assisting Barden at her dance studio. Billings plans to study architecture at Norwich University, while Needham will study child psychology and development at Southern New Hampshire University.

My wife and I worry often about the cultural pressures that seem to beleaguer teen girls these days, especially given how quickly our own daughter seems to be growing up. We have read about the eating disorders, the self-loathing, and the pressures to be popular and beautiful and wear suitably snug jeans. We have seen the statistics about teenage drug use and sex, and have shaken our heads ruefully.

But then we see young women like Billings and Needham, and we breathe massive sighs of relief. Yes, the high school hallways today might be filled with croptops and tattoos, and there are young women who define themselves solely in terms of their friends, their sexuality, or their cars.

There are also, however, teen girls who have transcended the stereotype and offer glorious role models for the children five and ten years behind them.

Earlier this month in a savvy *Newsweek* magazine cover story about the state of teen girls, writer Susannah Meadows outlined the three factors that seem to encourage confidence, independence, and emotional well-being:

- After-school activities

- Parents who are supportive and involved with their daughters

- A solid grounding in the family's religion

These might be common sense for many parents, but they are important and worth repeating.

Godspeed, girls. And thank you for being there for my daughter.

A PERSON CAN LEARN A LOT
FROM IAN FREEMAN

IAN FREEMAN'S coffee-colored hair is slicked back in an Elvis Presley pompadour. The fourteen-year-old has the late rock star's stage swagger down pat, as well as the Presley sneer: boyish and ingratiating one moment—the smile of a shy kid from Mississippi who doesn't quite understand what all the fuss is about—self-assured and almost roguish the next. The music begins, a series of vibrant guitar riffs, and girls race from their seats to the very edge of the stage, waving their arms and screaming. Freeman raises his eyebrows with a rock star's studied insouciance and twirls his microphone at these adoring fans. If you squint, it is almost possible to see the King strutting there on the boards, instead of a teenage boy with Down syndrome.

Ian is lip-synching to the music on a Thursday afternoon in an annual show in northwest Vermont in which all the acts feature performers with developmental disabilities. This year the show is in the Contois Auditorium, the modest theater in the city hall building in Burlington. I like the notion that the mayor of the state's largest city (by far) and most of the city administrators are working nearby: It adds a veneer of mainstream approval to a cabaret in which the mere fact that one of the performers is playing "Ode to Joy" on an electric organ matters far more than his technical prowess.

I've become friends with Ian because his mother and my nine-year-old daughter—both of whom are named Grace—are performing in a community theater together, and Ian, the two Graces, and I have been carpooling together two hours a day, four days a week, to rehearsals. The two Graces have voices and ranges that put Ian's and mine to shame when we sing together in the car, a reality that troubles Ian not at all and me, these days, only a bit.

Before I met Ian, I was sufficiently self-conscious that I would never have sung in the car.

Grace Freeman has been raising Ian entirely on her own since the boy was born. She has no other children. She and Ian's father broke up while Grace was pregnant—the two weren't married— and she had never expected there would be any co-parenting.

It is no easy task to be a single mother in even the best of circumstances, and it is particularly challenging when your child has Down syndrome. Ian also was born with a variety of other ailments that often accompany Down syndrome, including deafness and asthma. But Grace and Ian have been their own small world for almost a decade and a half now, and my sense is that if their little planet isn't perfect, in some ways it may spin more smoothly than the one on which most people roam. Ian is the first person with Down syndrome with whom I've become friends, and as I've gotten to know him it's become apparent that he has a good deal more to teach me than I am likely to teach him.

Ian and I and the two Graces are in a pizza parlor on our way to one of the first rehearsals for the show the females are in. Ian's mother is an elementary school teacher by day and an active member of a variety of community theater groups by night. When she isn't performing in a show, as she is now, she is likely to be a music director. Almost Ian's entire life he has been with her at rehearsals, and so he knows musicals the way some teenagers know MTV videos. His favorites at the moment are *The Secret Garden,* the show his mother just finished in Burlington, and *Once on This Island,* the show she is doing now in Stowe, Vermont. His ability to memorize entire librettos would be impressive with any child, but it is particularly striking given that Ian reads at a second-grade level and so he learns them largely through what he picks up with his hearing aids. (When I expressed, evidently with no small sense of wonder, Ian's uncanny ability to learn song lyrics to Kim Xidas of the National Association for Down Syndrome, she reminded me gently, "People with Down syndrome have gifts just like anyone else.")

While the four of us are in the booth in the restaurant waiting for our pizza to arrive—the girls on one side, Ian and me on the other—I am sipping a diet cola and Ian is drinking an orange soda.

"That looks good," I murmur, having not had an orange soda in years. His mother is cutting his pizza into small pieces for him.

"Try it!" he says, and pushes the glass over to me and starts to lean the straw toward my mouth.

I defer. I'm a pretty uptight guy: I don't share straws with anyone other than my wife and my daughter.

"Really, Chris, it's so good," Ian continues. "I want you to have some." Ian speaks quickly, and the combination of his deafness and Down syndrome means that it's difficult to understand precisely what he is saying. It sounds sometimes as if he is trying to speak with a soggy English muffin in his mouth. Ian's intent, however, his desire to share something that he cherishes with me, is clear. And so I reach for the straw he is aiming at my lips and take a sip. It is good—considerably sweeter than the diet stuff on which I subsist, and a comforting echo of soft drinks from my own adolescence—and I thank him. He nods, smiling. Then abruptly he wraps both arms around me in a ferociously affectionate bear hug and tells me that he loves me.

Even my brother and I have difficulty saying that to each other.

Roughly one out of every eight hundred to a thousand children is born with Down syndrome. The odds increase dramatically as a woman gets older: A twenty-year-old has a mere one in two thousand likelihood of giving birth to a baby with the genetic disorder; a forty-nine-year-old has a one in ten chance.

Grace Freeman was thirty-six when Ian was born. She had done no prenatal testing—no amniocentesis, no ultrasonography—both because she wanted a baby so badly and because there was no history of Down's in her family. She told herself it wasn't possible that her child might be born with a disability. Nevertheless, she admits that while she was pregnant she wondered sometimes if she was whistling in the dark, and she wasn't completely surprised when he was born with the syndrome: "I'd sensed something was wrong," she recalls. "I had no concrete reason to believe this, but Ian started moving around late, and when he moved, he just moved so slowly."

Down syndrome is named for John Langdon Down, the nineteenth-century British physician who described the characteristics of the condition and differentiated it from mental retardation. The condition is the result of a chromosomal abnormality: Instead of the normal forty-six chromosomes in each cell—twenty-two pairs, plus the two that determine gender—a person with Down syndrome has a forty-seventh. The vast majority of the time, that extra chromosome is linked to the twenty-first pair of chromosomes. The scientific term is the pleasant-sounding alliterative "trisomy 21."

Grace says she was devastated when, ten days after Ian was born, she received the news that the chromosome tests had indeed confirmed that her little boy had Down syndrome: "We were at my mom's, and I just went completely to pieces. I was beside myself. I remember people telling me that I had to have a funeral for the baby I didn't have—that perfectly healthy one."

People were also telling her that she should consider giving Ian up for adoption, that as a single mother she couldn't possibly raise him on her own.

"But I didn't have any doubt," she says. "I knew I could do it. I had two brothers and their wives here in Vermont, my mom and dad, a lot of cousins, and a niece living nearby. We'd get through this." Her mother has been her greatest support: From the very first meeting with a geneticist through Ian's five separate ear surgeries, invariably she has accompanied her daughter and grandson to his doctors' appointments. But Grace has also been helped enormously by her friends in Lincoln, the central Vermont village in which she and Ian live. When logistics prohibit her from bringing Ian with her to a rehearsal, neighbor Lisa Dobkowski will stay with Ian until she gets home; when an overnight class trip to the Children's Museum in Boston prevents her from returning to Vermont until the next day, Lisa's fourteen-year-old daughter, Emily, will spend the night in the guest room in the Freeman house. Other times Ian will have a sleepover with friends up the road. And, these days, Grace is comfortable leaving Ian home alone for hours at a time, making sure he understands that if he needs anything he should simply press the redial button on their cordless phone and, for instance, their friend Barb Aitken will pick up.

Once when Grace went to Burlington and left Ian alone, she had keyed the redial into their neighbors, the Pertas, where thirteen-year-old Amaia was home. That night when Grace returned, the teen girl said, her voice a combination of incredulity and wonder, that she and Ian must have spoken a hundred times that day. Ian loved the redial feature, and the nearly instant connection it offered.

Nevertheless, Grace insists that the real secret to raising Ian alone is that she is a "hyperactive workaholic overachiever." In addition to her job as a schoolteacher and the time she commits to community theater, she spends her Tuesday nights playing an African drum with a group of musicians and dancers. She and Ian have horses in the meadow behind their home, a pair of miniature Arabians. And their 175-year-old farmhouse itself is a steady home-improvement project, with Grace doing much of the work herself. Right now she is replacing the joists in the basement and strengthening the first floor.

Ian is in their den today when I arrive for a visit, meticulously acting out the first half of the 1997 blockbuster movie, *Titanic*. One moment he is Leonardo DiCaprio showing Kate Winslet how it feels to stand at the bowsprit of the massive ship as it plunges through the Atlantic waves, and the next he is trying hard to turn the vessel away from the iceberg that has appeared out of nowhere. He is so focused on his performance that easily fifteen minutes pass before he puts his head into the dining room where his mother and I are sitting to say hello. When he discovers I am there, however, instantly the movie is forgotten as he leads me upstairs to show me how he and his mother have rearranged things in the loft in his bedroom, then the exercise bike in the guest room, then the map of Massachusetts he has completed at school, then downstairs to the work his mother is doing in the basement, and then outside to visit Gypsy and Little Fellow, their horses.

Like his mother, Ian has a lot of energy.

Ian is short, as are many people with Down syndrome, but he's not that much smaller than I am. I am five-eight. Most of the time he dresses like the other teenagers at the public high school he attends, which these days means baggy blue jeans and T-shirts.

Unlike his peers, Ian will occasionally break a few fashion rules. Once when I went straight from the airport to meet my daughter at a rehearsal—I'd been out of town for five days—I arrived wearing the black sports jacket I had worn on the plane. Ian tried it on, rolling up the sleeves because my arms are longer than his, but the makeover was uncanny. We have, apparently, similar-size shoulders, and so with the sleeves cuffed the jacket fit nicely. Ian was transformed into a man before my eyes. His posture grew from the casual slouch typical of many teen boys to the erect posture of a foreign diplomat. He put his shoulders back, his chest forward, and positively strutted around the corners of the dance room where his mother and my daughter were rehearsing.

Ian is a chameleon—or, as Grace calls him, a mimic. He understands instinctively the maxim about clothes making the man, and loves costumes. After he saw *Joseph and the Amazing Technicolor Dreamcoat,* he would don the multicolored cloak his mother had made for him and parade around the house as Pharaoh. Currently, with his mother in *Once on This Island,* a musical that features four temperamental gods pulling the strings on a mystic Caribbean island, he is often costumed in the majestic robes worn by Agwe, the show's god of water.

In this production, Agwe is played by a young Vermont actor

named James Blanchard. James, twenty-three, and Ian have been friends since the two met when Ian's mom and James worked on another musical together, and James offers Ian one of the few things his mother can't: a male role model. It's one thing to stop with Mom for an ice cream after rehearsal; it's a considerably bigger deal to stop to have one with James.

In a blurring of worlds, however, Ian never calls him James. He always refers to him instead as the name of the character James is playing at that moment—Dr. Craven last season, Agwe this summer.

This evening James and the ensemble are learning the blocking and choreography for a song called "Rain," in which Agwe unleashes a fierce storm upon the island. The dance has broad arm movements, prayers and pleas, and some very fluid dancing. The choreographer is moving quickly because there is a lot to cover. Nevertheless, standing there between the lip of the stage and the front row of seats is Ian, watching Agwe carefully and mirroring precisely the way the water god lets loose a tempest.

When the actors finally take a break, James sits down with Ian and teaches him precisely how Agwe will summon the squall.

"Ian has a natural theatrical bent, and so he loves to recite my lines with me. But basically we just play together the way I might play with any children in the cast. We goof around, we have fun," James says. Then, after considering Ian a moment, he adds—his voice rising slightly in wonder—"He has to be one of the most cheerful people I've ever met."

So long as Ian's mother is in a show with an Agwe or a Dr. Craven—or any of the other stage dads who've passed through his life—the teenager doesn't seem unduly concerned by his father's absence.

———

My wife wonders what it says about our world that it's the people among us with the lower IQs who hug unashamedly and love unconditionally. Ian is the only teenage boy either of us knows, including our nephews, who actually wants to embrace people.

These days I'm a theater person because my daughter is a theater person. But I've noticed as I chauffeur my Grace to the different shows she's been in that theater people hug, too. They hug even me, and all I do is drive one of the cast members to rehearsals because she's seven years shy of her driver's license.

Consequently, Ian is in his element in his mother's community of actors and dancers and singers. He may never play Tony in *West Side Story,* but someday he might lip-synch "Something's Coming" and make us imagine, for a moment, Richard Beymer's fiery gaze and fervent conviction that he has a miracle in his future. He may never reprise Mandy Patinkin's Broadway performance as Archibald Craven in *The Secret Garden,* but he sure can belt it out in the car.

Me, too—at least when I am with Ian. When we're driving to rehearsals together, I handle Neville Craven's songs and Ian sings brother Archie's. The two Graces are responsible for the women around them. And though I realize that my singing voice hovers between laughable and appalling—I am incapable of either carrying or distinguishing notes—my inhibitions slide away when I'm around Ian. I succumb completely to the boy's energy and enthusiasm and spectacular joy in the moment.

Certainly there is a long litany of things that Ian will never do in this life, but that's true for us all. Unlike many of us, however, Ian makes people happy—and that is a mighty accomplishment for anyone.

THE
LOCAL WILDLIFE

SURLY COW DISPLAYS NO REMORSE

SOME YEARS AGO, my wife and I were driving south through Hinesburg on a foggy night in the spring, when out of the mist came a herd of cows in the road, charging north. We stopped the car and prepared for death, and then watched as the animals ran past us on both sides.

When the animals were well behind us and the ground had stopped shaking, we exited the car and started screaming and hollering as loud as we could. The farmers who were chasing the cows were yelling too, and so they thought we were trying to help corral the cows back into the barn where they belonged. This made for a perfectly fine arrangement: We could shriek, the cows could run, and everyone got a much-needed cardiovascular workout.

In all fairness, I actually did wave my arms a bit at the cows and try to push a few in the general direction of the barn. A number of times I even explained that I was a vegetarian, but obviously these cows were female, and they knew they were in no danger of becoming Quarter Pounders.

Eventually we got the cows home, and we did so without spilling any milk on either the asphalt or our car's fender.

I did learn a valuable lesson that night, however: Cows can be ornery.

Farmers, of course, learn this at an early age. Cows can be surly. Cows can be stubborn. Cows can be stupid.

And so I think it speaks volumes about Curt Estey that he has

110 cows on his Bristol dairy farm, and there is only one with whom he has a somewhat contentious relationship: No. 26.

Now No. 26 isn't huge, but she's 1,300 pounds of solid Holstein. She offers roughly sixty pounds of milk a day, and the amount is steadily climbing. She's an admirable producer.

And she's good to look at: cow eyes as deep as precious stones, a nose that looks like a scoop of blackberry sorbet. When she lows, her moo is a cross between a foghorn and the alto in a more than adequate choir.

But No. 26 grew testy during the last trimester of her pregnancy this spring. It was the first time she was with calf, and she grew demanding in unattractive ways. She grew piggy. Mulish. Downright bullheaded.

The folks on the farm found themselves steering clear of the cow. They couldn't wait for her to become de-calfeinated.

Finally, in early May, No. 26 exploded. She was eight months pregnant, and she'd had it with mud and Curt and the other cows. She'd had it with being an animal that had to cram four stomachs and a baby inside her. And so while Curt was training her to enter the milking parlor, she became a one-woman World Wrestling Federation wrecking crew. A Bovine Boxer. The Great Holstein Hope.

One moment she was a cow and the next she was a blur, slamming Curt into the wall of the barn, and breaking two of his ribs.

Now this was not the first time that Curt had had his ribs broken on the farm. A scant thirty yards from the spot in the barn where No. 26 had hip-checked him into the boards, a tractor had toppled upon him when he was eleven.

This was by far, however, his most painful accident, because the cow in question has shown absolutely no contrition.

"I've seen no evidence there's any guilt inside her," Estey says, "and that's very troubling. I've seen no sign of regret."

Moreover, No. 26 has now had her calf, and the farmer has yet to witness any indication that the new mother will instill even the most rudimentary sense of right and wrong in her progeny.

Consequently, I called a variety of people who've spent their lives around cows to see if No. 26 was typical of the species: Hard-hearted. Amoral. Quick to anger, slow to remorse.

The sad news? No. 26 is not merely typical, she may be quintessential. Said retired Lincoln farmer Fletcher Brown, "How difficult are cows? Why, they're as bad as some people!"

DEAD BAT DUTY DRAWS THE LINE

IF YOU ARE among the especially strong-stomached who occasionally read this column over Sunday breakfast or brunch, stop eating. Right now. Chew whatever is in your mouth, swallow, and push your chair away from the table.

OK. Ready?

There is a dead bat inside my woodstove. It looks glued to the inside of the door, its little bat head half-buried in the wrought-iron damper, its little bat body pressed flush against the creosote paste. Its furry bat back has upon it what I believe is a furry bat fungus.

I would tell you more about what the dead bat looks like, but I can't look at it long enough to give you the sort of idiosyncratic details of decomposition that might bring this piece to—forgive the irony—life.

See, the bat's been there since Labor Day.

No, that's not true. I discovered it Labor Day, but for all I know, it has been there since the Fourth of July.

It's still hanging upside-down inside my woodstove because I am dead-bat-removal-challenged. As a matter of fact, I'm pretty much any dead-animal-removal-challenged, but bats are especially problematic for me.

This is because a bat looks like a small flying rodent that happens to move at supersonic speed, while squeaking like a bath toy on crack.

And as my friend Ron Rood says about bats in his book, *Animals Nobody Loves,* most bats have a face "as endearing as a Halloween mask" (which makes me especially glad the dead bat in my woodstove decided to auger into the wall face first).

My sense is that removing the bat would be a relatively less stomach-turning proposition if the animal were simply dead on the woodstove floor. I'd simply adapt the method I use to remove dead mice in the attic, and push Mr. Bat Cadaver into Mr. Paper Bag with a stick, and then run like an Olympic sprinter to the Dumpster next door.

The bat in the woodstove, however, presents a (gulp) stickier problem. Given the way the little fellow clings to the door, I have a feeling I'll need either a spatula to scrape him from the side, or spaghetti tongs to yank him off it.

I may be wrong, but I've yet to find the courage to find out.

In any case, the arrival of Carcass the Bat in our woodstove has precipitated a lot of discussion in the house about sex-role socialization, the different responsibilities of women and men, and the proper division of labor in the modern home.

In other words, my wife and I have had a lot of conversations that have begun, "Chris, would you please get rid of that indescribably horrible, grotesque piece of yuck in the wood-stove?"

My wife is, by any definition, a feminist. Right now her nightstand has on it—this is not column-driven hyperbole—books by Susan Faludi, Jill Ker Conway, and Kate Millett.

It's clear, however, that in our household, disposing of dead bats remains man's work. I don't know why this is . . .

Oh, who am I kidding, I know exactly why this is. It's because the dead bat smells like cheese at the beach in August, and looks like roadkill too repulsive for crows.

Consequently, at some point soon I will have to overcome the fact I am dead-bat-removal-challenged. I will have to find the courage to get the spatula or the tongs or perhaps even the little fireplace shovel and murmur, "Ashes to ashes, dust to . . ."

Or, perhaps not. It's September, the nights are chilly. Perhaps I should be grateful to the bat for choosing to die where he did.

Perhaps it's time for the first wood fire of the year. Little bat . . . tiny flitter mouse . . . baby chiropteran . . . Can you say "cremation"?

TOWN'S ALL ATWITTER ABOUT ROSIE

FOR A FEW days last month, all anyone was chirping about at the Lincoln General Store was Rosalita Poplawski's hysterectomy.

Sometimes, if the group assembled around the coffee machine was male, the conversation would be couched in euphemism ("I think it's a woman problem"), but other times the twitter would focus on how the family was coping: "How's her sister doing? She worried? How about Teo?"

Once, I overheard an analysis of Rosalita's methods of contraception. "I don't get it," someone observed. "If she's on birth control, why does she keep laying eggs?"

Why indeed? Until last month, Rosalita was laying about twenty eggs a year, a total that probably wouldn't impress a chicken, but isn't half bad for a cockatiel. Her sister, Isabella, lays about the same number.

The two birds are five years old, their coloring a combination of soft yellows and orange. Sometimes Rosalita sports a letter or two on her head, a result of descending from her perch to the bottom of the cage and burrowing under the floor made from newspaper (though never, of course, this newspaper).

The birds are small, about six inches long exclusive of the tail feathers that trail behind them like a wedding dress train. They live in the Sparks-Poplawski household in Lincoln: Rosalita belongs to Teo, seven, and Isabella to Nicholas, eleven.

Until recently, they were the sort of robust birds that would fly happily around the inside of the Sparks-Poplawski home, landing contentedly on the children's fingers, the parents' heads, and dropping birdie-poop smart bombs wherever they wanted.

About three months ago, however, Nicholas and Teo's mother, Becky, noticed that Rosalita's squeaks were weak, and she was holding onto the cage with her bill.

And so she took Rosalita to the Shelburne Veterinary Hospital, which was a relatively easy task, except for the fact it was twenty below zero, and Rosalita is a Latino cockatiel—which means she prefers a slightly warmer climate than polar tundra. Becky warmed up the car for a long time, and put Rosalita in her birdie transport, a cat carrier.

The veterinarians, Dr. Ross Prezant and Dr. Steven Metz, diagnosed the problem right away: egg jam. A cockatiel egg is roughly as big as a good-sized marble, which isn't big at all unless you're a cockatiel and the egg is doing an internal imitation of an ice jam in March.

Consequently, Prezant performed surgery: He broke the egg. By Christmas Day it was clear Rosalita would live, and by the Tuesday after Christmas she was home.

In the third week of January, however, the ailment returned: Oval Ovum Entrapment. Once again, Prezant extracted the egg. In addition, this time the doctor put Rosalita on birdie birth control—a protocol that might, at first, strike anyone who isn't relentlessly optimistic as a tad unnecessary, given the fact that Rosalita's only birdie buddy is female, too.

Ah, but these are unfertilized eggs. Hence the avis prophylactic.

Did the contraception work? Nope. Early last month, for the third time since December 23, the veterinarian had to perform an emergency egg-in-dectomy on Rosalita. Once more the cockatiel lived, but it was clear to Rosalita's family that the little bird's eyes were, so to speak, bigger than its stomach. Something had to be done.

And so on February 12, for the fourth time in his career, Prezant got out his teeny-tiny scalpel and his miniature clamps, and attempted a bird hysterectomy. Now, bird surgery is dicey. Not only are the organs diminutive, but a bird can only withstand anesthesia for somewhere between fifteen and thirty minutes. Consequently, a doctor has to work fast, with little room for error.

Teo remembers spending a long chunk of that day simply murmuring to herself over and over, "Please-please-please-please-please."

Her pleas were answered. Rosalita came out of surgery just fine, and today the family is, understandably, all atwitter. Especially Isabella.

And the patrons at the Lincoln General Store learned once again that, if you want to make an omelet, you have to break some eggs.

IT'S NOT MIND OVER MATTER— IT'S MIND OVER MANURE

THIS AUTUMN I fell off a horse for the first time. I've been riding for three years, and so I was due.

I was cantering in a rutted field dotted with spindly apple trees and a few boulders the size of Volkswagens, and one second the horse and I were paralleling a fence by a road, and the next I was on the ground looking up at him as he snitched leaves off a tree beside us. I was—and this seems all too appropriate—directly beside a fresh pile of poop left by one of his pals from the stable where I ride.

Falling was a humbling experience, though not because I have ever deluded myself for even a nanosecond that I have the slightest idea what I'm doing when I'm on a horse. I only started riding because I was researching the experience for a book, and because it struck me as one more hobby I could share with my daughter as she grew up. We ride together once a week. Over time, however, I discovered how much pleasure I, too, was deriving from riding: the sense of power and speed, the feeling of accomplishment, the reality that here was another way to indulge the mid-life demons that besiege a man once he is forty.

No, falling was troubling for the simple reason that it revealed to me just how in thrall our bodies are to our minds. (As Yogi Berra is alleged to have said about baseball, "It's ninety percent mental. The other half is physical.")

Without wanting to subject anyone—least of all myself—to some completely ill-advised and uninformed armchair psychotherapy, I believe I fell in part because on the way to the stable I'd been listening on the car radio to actor Christopher Reeve discuss his new book, *Nothing Is Impossible,* on *Fresh Air* with Terry Gross.

It is difficult to think of Reeve without recalling the tragic equestrian accident in 1995 that left him a quadriplegic. This was especially true that afternoon because he and Gross were discussing both what he cannot do and the small but astonishing strides he has made as a result of vigorous physical therapy.

And so as I tacked up the horse I kept imagining that moment years ago when Reeve was thrown from his mount. And then I saw over and over in my mind the loop of film from *Gone With the Wind* when little Bonnie Blue Butler takes a header off her small but energetic pony and dies.

I was riding alone that day on a stallion named J.T. I like J.T. a lot, and not simply because he's the only male at the stable who is—and I will try to be delicate about this—intact. J.T. is an aging Morgan show horse, whose moniker is short for "Justin Time." I think the world of this animal because he has a kind disposition with inept riders like me, and because he still loves to run. I've ridden him almost exclusively this year.

And then out of the blue I fell. I won't say I was thrown because that would imply J.T. was culpable, and it's clear this was my fault—not his. He stayed right beside me, a further indication that he hadn't meant to rocket me into space.

But topple I did, and my back and neck were sore for a week. When I climbed back upon J.T. that day, I did so with the grace and agility of a very old man.

I don't view riding as any more dangerous than skiing, snowmobiling, or most of the myriad ways we humans entertain ourselves. I wouldn't encourage my daughter to ride if I did. Moreover, I've had a splendid afternoon every time I've ridden J.T. since that tumble. Nevertheless, I remain struck by the way a small quiver of fear in the back of my mind sent me over the top of a horse. Apparently riding, too, is ninety percent mental. The other half's physical.

THE CASE OF THE CURIOUS CRUSTACEAN

NO ONE LIKES roadkill. No one likes seeing it, driving by it, eating it, and—especially—causing it.

And while even a PETA-dues-paying vegetarian weenie like me understands that roadkill is one of those undeniable harbingers of spring, I am careful to focus my seasonal reveries of rebirth upon the bluebird, the dandelion, and the sugarhouse steam.

Let's face it: There is little poetry in roadkill.

There is probably a message lurking somewhere here, but to be frank, it was neither moral outrage nor a yen for a tofu substitute for opossum pudding that inspired it.

Rather, it was a lobster.

Last month I was returning to Vermont from Boston. Midmorning, in the wooded stretch of Interstate 89 that rolls like waves between Concord and West Lebanon, in the breakdown lane to my right, I saw my first road-killed crustacean.

At first I thought it was a plastic toy by the way the sun bounced off its shell, or perhaps a "happy meal" lunch box from Red Lobster.

I slowed down to study it more closely, although I don't usually find my daughter her new toys along the side of the road—unless, of course, what happens to be lurking there is a sandbox with a big "Make me an offer!" sign.

What led me to stop? Well, one reason was the fact my car windows were up: Had my windows been down, the smell from the roadside attraction alone would have kept me speeding along at a steady sixty-five.

In any case, I climbed from the car, tried to breathe solely through my mouth, and stood for a moment in awe: It was a lobster all right, probably a good one-and-a-half to two pounds of shellfish.

And, I'm sorry to say, the stench was a pretty fair indication that its heart was beating-challenged, its pincers were gripper-challenged, and its legs were movement-challenged.

The animal, in short, was living-challenged.

It's no mystery how a raccoon winds up inside-out by the side of the road.

But a lobster? This was a mystery. Its claws were not rubber-banded as if it were a grocery lobster cavalierly tossed from a speeding car window. And its eyes, though lifeless, didn't look like they'd ever had that death-row gaze lobsters get after days in a holding tank.

And so I made some inquiries. I began with Vermont's Department of Fish and Wildlife, asking law-enforcement assistant Maureen Allen how she thought the lobster had arrived on I-89.

Her theory? First of all, she convinced me it didn't swim there, pointing out that lobsters need more salt in their water than even a highway department drops on a road.

Then she suggested the lobster had either been left there accidentally by someone selling the animal's lobster friends by the side of the road, or someone had left the creature on the hood of his car and then sped off, leaving the shellfish in the dust.

"You wouldn't think anyone would put a lobster on the hood of his car, but you wouldn't think anyone would put a purse there either. But people do that all the time," she said.

Then I called the Net Result, a Burlington seafood store. Heather Wyman actually deepened the mystery when she explained that lobsters don't generally swim, they crawl—meaning the fact I was inland didn't matter!

And, she said, lobsters can live up to three days from the ocean, if they're properly wrapped in moist seaweed or newspaper.

So, is it conceivable this lobster had a reason for crawling north, and somewhere along the way lost its seaweed slicker? As they say on *Unsolved Mysteries,* "No one knows for sure."

I think, however, my favorite theory belongs to my wife, who has spent many hours lately with her nose buried in children's books: "A great but greedy bird scooped the lobster from the sea and carried him over land until he grew too heavy. And so the bird had to drop him, despite his days and days of effort."

AN OLD CAT'S NAME ALONE
CONJURED WONDROUS MEMORIES

EARLIER THIS SUMMER, my wife, my daughter, and I said good-bye to one of our cats, an animal who lived exactly one season shy of seventeen years. Merlin—a male with dime-a-dozen black-and-white tuxedo markings—was named by my wife and me for the minister who married us, Leslie Merlin, because he was found on our wedding day.

For the past four years, we were giving Merlin two shots a day for diabetes, and for the past eighteen months we were insisting that he swallow a half tablet of children's Benadryl in the morning and then another half in the evening so he could breathe without wheezing like a fireplace bellows.

Merlin was one of four cats in our house, but he was my wife's and my first together, and he outlasted enough feline sisters and brothers to fill a small wall of cages at an animal shelter. He lived longer than Cassandra, who we will remember for many things, not the least of which was the time she hid for a weekend on the top shelf of my closet when my wife and I were away and—unwilling to come down—sprinkled urine like rain down upon all my blazers and suits.

He saw B.K.—a.k.a. Barn Kitty—come and go, the first of many cats who discovered that the couple who lived in Lincoln in the yellow house with the yellow barn next to the church could be counted on for free food and medical care, and just maybe a spot by the woodstove. When I recall B.K., I think of a Tuesday before Thanksgiving, when my wife came home from the supermarket and left a good-sized turkey on the front porch along with a couple of bags of groceries. B.K. had both the strength and the brazen self-confidence to nose the rock-hard bird down the porch steps and then try to drag it back to the barn.

Merlin outlived his closest feline friend, Clinton. Clinton, another stray, was named for the Brooklyn street on which we found him, not our former president. On the other hand, there were evenings when—not unlike the junior U.S. senator from New York—I did imagine standing outside and yelling for Clinton to stop tomcatting around the neighborhood and come home.

Merlin saw Ranger, another barn cat, come and go (and, truly, we do not know where that great wanderer finally went), and he lived longer by far than Matilda.

He outlasted the dogs in the nearby houses who occasionally chased him—Fred and Alice and Barney—as well as my mother and my father-in-law, and the grandparents who attended my wife's and my wedding.

Merlin leaves behind three feline siblings, all younger things whom he tolerated with varying degrees of haughtiness and magisterial indifference. He was, without question, the smartest cat we have had, as well as the most persnickety: He demanded a pristine litter box and then, in his later years, his very own litter box. Unlike his less-entitled peers who migrated into our home from the barn, he would actually turn up his nose at select brands and flavors of cat food. And he always took the warmest spot on the porch or the shadiest spot under the irises.

It might be wrong to have favorites among our pets, especially since our pets are in large measure what we make of them: They represent parts of our lives, iconic shorthands and Rorschach tests, and their names alone often conjure who we were when we first took them in.

Nevertheless, that is precisely the reason why I will miss seeing Merlin and saying his name. He was my wife's and my first cat together, and the one who could remind us both of our wedding day. Even when he was a very old man, when we would pet him or feed him or hold him in our lap while giving him his twice-a-day Benadryl, he could remind us both of what it was like to be young.

THE GREEN—
AND THEN
SPECTACULARLY
YELLOW AND RED—
MOUNTAINS

WHY THE GREEN MOUNTAINS
TURN RED

I AM STANDING in the remains of a turret in Scotland's Edzell Castle, staring down into the restored Renaissance garden that a British nobleman designed four hundred years ago. This castle is a gem: It has the power of history (Mary, Queen of Scots, visited here), the aura that permeates any relic the size of a football field, and a vast garden with roses, statuary, and hedgerows trimmed to spell out the inspirational motto of the Clan Lindsay, when seen from above.

When the British couple beside me hear that I hail from Vermont, however, the subject turns instantly to leaves. Specifically, it turns to Vermont leaves. An elderly French couple quickly chime in, wanting to share their memories of a September visit to the Green Mountains in 1979 and how they had never seen anything like the Vermont foliage. I try to steer the conversation back to the castle in which we are standing, but in the opinion of these four Europeans, the Vermont autumn is infinitely more interesting than a castle built centuries ago.

The Vermont foliage is like that: For two or three weeks in late September and early October, the trees explode in an absolutely phantasmagoric display of color. The maples—a third of the trees in the state—turn shades of crimson and cherry and red, the birches become an almost neon yellow, and the ash becomes a purple that is as flamboyant as my young daughter's most vibrant Magic Marker. The color moves inexorably from north to south, from the higher to the lower elevations, traveling through the trees like a tsunami.

And along with those colors come the leaf peepers. Roughly four million people visit Vermont in the autumn, almost seven times the state's population—spending close to a billion dollars, according to the state's tourism department. Several upscale bed-and-breakfast owners tell me they are likely to do a sixth of their annual business during that three-week period when the leaves may be at their best.

Moreover, while the tourists may be visiting in large measure because of the foliage, it's not merely the colors in the trees that have drawn them: It's the notion that the whole Vermont landscape is a throwback, an unspoiled glimpse of agrarian America. The dairy farm may be beleaguered in Vermont, but some 1,600 still remain, and it is easy to find a hillside speckled with Holsteins or discover a red barn beside an elegant country skyscraper of a silo. Though the woods don't feel exactly primeval, there are numerous pockets in the state where the trees still grow thick and the daylight can disappear. And while we do have Wal-Mart now—four, in fact—we also have iconic New England greens surrounded by white clapboard churches with elongated steeples, nineteenth-century Greek Revival "cottages" with slate roofs and gingerbread trim, and Victorian homes that boast fish-scale woodwork along their front porches.

Yet there is an irony to the foliage display the Vermont woods offers its guests every year, as well as to the notion that the state's remarkably beautiful landscape is the product of centuries of careful husbandry of the countryside. First, Vermonters almost completely deforested the state not once but twice in the last two-hundred years; second, if we hadn't leveled the forests, it is unlikely that our hillsides now would be exploding with myriad shades of red and yellow and orange.

I grew up loathing leaves. I was raised in the sort of mannered New England suburb in which lawns were supposed to be appropriately manicured every day of the year when they weren't buried in snow, and so I spent a great many September and October weekends as a child trying to keep up with the waves of leaves that would fall to their death between our house and the cul-de-sac on which we lived. (Autumn leaves to an elementary school student must be something like the mail in December to a postal worker: The leaves just keep falling and falling, and no sooner is the yard clean than a wind in the night blankets the ground with them once again.)

Consequently, it's probably no accident that my wife and I bought a house with few trees when we moved to a village in central Vermont. There are exactly two maple trees in our front yard, and two more on the edge of our driveway. With the exception of a pair of lilacs, all the trees we have planted in the fifteen years we have lived here are evergreens.

But I do love the magic of the Vermont foliage. Our house faces Mount Abraham and Mount Ellen, and the color is indeed spectacular. If there hasn't been an early snow in the higher elevations, closing the gap road through the mountains, the tour buses filled with leaf peepers will drive right past my home. The autumnal exhibit in my village is so extravagant that five Septembers ago Priscilla Presley was here with a forty-person crew and a European advertising agency to film a television commercial for Indian Summer perfume. The European director wanted perfect foliage, and the location scouts chose a dirt road and a strip of woods just south of the town. The crew's cell phones wouldn't work in our hills, and they had to depend on the lone rotary phone in the local general store—a situation that probably went from quaint to annoying between days one and four of their visit—but otherwise the shoot was successful. The leaves were particularly brilliant that year.

I had lived in Vermont for a decade before I learned from my friend John Elder that my state's autumn beauty is the inadvertent result of man's natural rapaciousness. Elder teaches in both the English and environmental studies departments at Middlebury College. The two of us were hiking throughout the Bristol Cliffs Wilderness Area and talking about the book he was then writing about Robert Frost's appreciation for this section of the state.

Although the steep woods were thick and the trees were tall, Elder showed me the places where the woods had been logged a century earlier and the oxen had pulled the fallen timber from the forest. There, on the trunk of an old birch, were the remains of an iron cable. Once that cable would have been attached to the yoke of the oxen, so that if the animals slipped, they wouldn't tumble down the hill to their deaths.

His point? The trees around us were barely eighty years old.

Most of Vermont is like that. Despite two rounds of deforestation that laid the state bare, Vermont is now seventy-eight percent forest. Originally, man obliterated much of the forest at the end of the eighteenth century to make potash for gunpowder and soap and to fuel iron forges. Then, once the land was cleared, it was kept free for the merino sheep that energized the economy through the Civil War. Vermont, however, was never great sheep country.

In reality, it has never been great farming country. The land is hilly, the soil is rocky, and the climate can be ornery. After the Civil War, both the people and the sheep left, often following the new railroads west, and trees returned to the meadows and pastures—though this time the hardwoods returned in slightly greater numbers.

Still, even those trees didn't last long. The Vermonters who remained carved out a living any way they could, and that often meant logging. Despite the pleas of some of the first conservationists, the hillsides were soon cleared once again. Fortunately for leaf peepers, however, hardwoods like maple grow faster than pine. In torn, muddy ground no longer shielded from the sun by evergreens, the maple seeds took root and the trees quickly flourished. The configuration of the forest changed, with the result that the woods here comprise far more hardwoods and far fewer evergreens than two hundred years ago, and flatlanders have a reason to visit.

A dead leaf—even a magnificent specimen from a healthy red maple—is of little value. Preschoolers may trace its iconic fjords and bays and stencil upon its topographic veins; idiosyncratic interior designers may shellac clusters of them onto walls and boxes and place mats. The reality, however, is this: Once a leaf has fallen from a tree, it is well on its way toward decomposition. Either it will become a part of the carpet of humus that covers the forest floor (cuisine at the very bottom of the food chain), or it will be raked (often by an exasperated elementary school student). A leaf, like the rest of us, loses its looks real fast after death.

Yet unlike the rest of us—combinations of cells, animals or plants, it doesn't matter—the leaves that make up the Vermont hillsides die dazzlingly beautiful deaths. That is, in essence, what we are watching when we gaze at the annual autumnal fireworks in the trees: We are watching leaves die.

The tree is preparing for winter, and a part of its process is the elimination of all those dainty leaves that are ill-equipped to endure the oncoming cold. The tree does so by slowly producing a layer of cells at the base of the leaf, thereby preventing fluids from reaching it.

The leaves, meanwhile, stop producing chlorophyll—the chemical necessary for photosynthesis, the process by which a leaf uses sunlight to generate food. Chlorophyll is also the reason a leaf has such a rich green luster. When the chlorophyll is gone, however, the colors in the other chemicals (which have, of course, been there all along) become visible: the scarlet carotenoids of the maple tree, for example.

That beautiful red leaf, in other words, is slowly starving to death.

Often, leaf peepers (and the thousands of businesses that depend upon them) worry about the summer weather and what effect it will have on the timing of the color. In reality, weather has little effect: An unusually hot, dry summer might put some stress on the trees and may cause the foliage to peak two or three days earlier than usual; conversely, a cooler summer with plenty of moisture and clouds, like the one we just had, might prolong it an extra half-week. But these swings are marginal: Leaves change because the days are growing shorter, and there is no variability there.

Sometimes weather can affect the brilliance of the foliage—a drought can certainly dull the colors, just as sufficient moisture in the soil will enhance them—but again, rainfall is a relatively small factor. The leaves are going to turn, and it will almost always be a remarkable spectacle to watch—especially when it's part of a massive ribbon of color on a hill, with either a dairy farm or Norman Rockwell–esque village green in the foreground.

Douglas Mack, the chef and co-owner of Mary's at Baldwin Creek, a Bristol bed-and-breakfast with an award-winning restaurant attached, believes that it is exactly this combination of natural beauty and archetypal New England imagery that generates such devotion to the state. "There's a decided homeyness that comes with crisp autumn air, the changing leaves, and a fire in the fireplace. It's like coming home," he says. "Suddenly, your marriage looks wonderful and your kids have turned out OK. That's really what we're serving up here."

And that might be exactly why it touches some people more than the view of a garden from an ancient castle keep. The leaves signal the onset of winter and the desire in us all to cocoon in a place that is warm, cozy, and reminiscent of something called home.

VERMONT READY TO BE MIRED
IN SPRING

THE ROAD TO the center of Lincoln coils uphill for exactly 3.4 miles from Vermont 116. According to West Lincoln's Art Pixley, it has been paved for forty-eight years. Pixley, sixty, has lived on the road since he was four and sold peas from his garden to the road crew when he was twelve.

Before that road was paved, he says, leaving the mountain in March or April was an adventure.

Apparently, however, so was simply crossing the street.

Until she was married, Wanda Goodyear lived just east of the village, on the south side of Lincoln's main road. Goodyear has six children, thirteen grandchildren, and five great-grandchildren. A sizable number of our esteemed citizens might not be here today if one of Wanda's neighbors hadn't been home when she made the mistake of trying to traverse the street in the midst of mud season one day when she was six.

"I was on my way to the grist mill across the street, and the road was just complete mud. The mud must have been at least to my knees, and I got so stuck that I couldn't lift my legs. So there I was, smack in the middle of the road, unable to move. Finally I just started hollering. Fortunately, a fellow down the street heard me and was able to lift me out. He carried me home on his shoulders, as I recall."

Asphalt is one of the astonishing conveniences we take for granted—not unlike electricity. Just as the monumental ice storm this winter gave many of us an opportunity to experience life without Edison's brightest idea, the imminent arrival of mud season will give us the chance to brave the world before blacktop.

And what a world it is. A sizable portion of the roads in Vermont are still dirt: Quaint stuff on a dusty August afternoon, downright magic when the foliage is right in the fall. But in April or March, a dirt road becomes a quagmire.

Pixley says that when he was a boy, one of the principal north-south routes in Lincoln, Quaker Street, was simply called "the Mud Road."

I can understand why: My powerful Plymouth Colt (now long out to pasture) once got stuck so deep in Quaker Street slop that I had to climb out the window to escape. I considered leaving the vehicle where it was as a public service, figuring other cars could drive over the roof. The metal might be slippery, but at least it would offer a solid island in the midst of that muck.

As recently as thirty years ago, Clara Hallock and her husband, Ken, would have to stop where the Quaker Street asphalt comes to an end and pull off the road to wrap their tires in chains before turning right and trying to scale Bagley Hill.

Floyd Hall, who moved to Lincoln in 1936, can't begin to count the number of cars he's helped yank from the mud but guesses the figure must have three digits.

"A Model A had a twenty-one-inch tire," Hall says, "and the running board would be about two-thirds of the way up the tire. Before we paved the roads, it wasn't uncommon to see a car sunk in to the running board."

Getting stuck in the mud could happen to anyone, and it did. Blacktop and four-wheel drive and tires that tower over toddlers make it less likely today than a generation ago, but cars still get beached in our bogs.

Nevertheless, there's something to be said for the smell of spring that comes with that slop. It's uplifting and earthy, and it rises up from the ground on moist air. Often, it comes with the sound of frogs and birds you haven't heard in two seasons.

So while I certainly wouldn't encourage anyone to try to navigate a dirt road over the next month, the fact remains there's something to be said for experiencing our back country highways the way our grandparents did—before asphalt made local travel less full of surprises.

SPIRITS LIVE AT BARTLETT'S
SWIMMING HOLE

SOMETIMES WE FORGET how powerful the New Haven River is as it surges west along the road linking Bristol and Lincoln.

We know it's there, the asphalt aligned with the aqua, even when the trees that separate the road and the river are as lush as they are right this moment. But we tend not to focus upon the waterway's colossal power, or the fact its current is so pronounced and its falls so prominent that it was powering a hydroelectric plant in Bristol until 1959.

At the site of the river's most impressive natural drop, Bartlett's Falls, there once was a dam and a pipe, called a penstock, that funneled the water downriver to the generating station just north of Bristol. The dam and key parts of the penstock were all but obliterated by the hurricane of 1938.

It's not possible to live in the eastern half of Addison County and not know about Bartlett's. Today it's a swimming hole, and on summer afternoons, it is packed: a Coney Island at the base of a steep embankment thick with maple and pine and ash.

In the mornings, however, it is empty, and that's when I like to visit. It's not that I am misanthropic. But there is history at Bartlett's, and it's easier to feel its presence when the only sound is the falls.

In all fairness, of course, that sound is loud. Bartlett's is shaped a bit like the Canadian section of Niagara Falls. Horizontally, it is a wide, shallow horseshoe, which means it acts as a natural amphitheater. It exaggerates the already impressive sound of the water as it cascades a good thirty feet into the basin below.

Unlike Niagara, however, the water doesn't fall like drapes. Rather, it drops upon no fewer than six ledges as it makes its way down. Instead of one roiling mass of spray at the base, the air around Bartlett's is filled top to bottom with mist.

The remains of the dam are visible on both sides of the river, clusters of cement stanchions upon which one can sit in astonishing comfort.

These days, the stanchion on the southern shore has the words "Divers Beware!" written in bold letters because it is unsafe to dive off those ledges or supports: Earlier this summer, one young man died doing just that.

People also have died simply swimming near Bartlett's, especially little children. Lincoln's Bill James can't drive past the spot without thinking about the four-year-old son of friends from Rhode Island who drowned there. And Bristol's Jack Wendel can still recall the little girl who was caught in a nearby penstock close to sixty-five years ago, and died in the pipe under the water.

The great irony of that hurricane of 1938 is not that it washed away a dam or a penstock built at the end of the nineteenth century, but that it annihilated the improvements made with enormous effort at the end of the winter a mere six months earlier.

Some of the workers who constructed the new intake valve at Bartlett's had boarded at Wendel's house when he was a boy, and he remains amazed at the work they did in those still-frigid waters.

Yet Bartlett's is by no means a sad place, especially when the sun and the heat and the acoustics conspire to make it a classic Vermont swimming hole.

But when you visit Bartlett's alone, it feels different than when there's a crowd. Sit in a spot in the shade, and it is dark no matter where the sun is in the sky. It is never quiet there, thanks to the falls, but it can be very still. The falls drown out the sound of most animals, and without birds or chipmunks or squirrels, it seems as though you're completely alone.

And if you do stay out of the sun, Bartlett's grows chilly fast.

In August, of course, that chill can be welcome. It is not only a respite from the heat: It is a reminder of the stories that live on in our ruins.

THE VERMONT WOODS LOOK
DIFFERENT WITHOUT ANY LEAVES

RECENTLY I HELD a rifle in my hands and went hunting.

Actually, that's not completely true: I walked around the woods a lot with an unloaded eight-and-a-half-pound gun slung over my shoulder and sat for a long time on a snow-covered boulder the size of a school bus.

My friend, Lincoln's Bob Patterson, was doing the hunting. Most of the day I was simply trying to make as little noise as possible and to figure out how to tell Bob that I needed to mark a tree really badly, but given the amount of buck urine we were wearing I was concerned this would undermine our efforts.

Deer, apparently, have a pretty good sense of smell, and

would be able to tell from anything I happened to leave on a beech tree that there was a human in the woods who had eaten Lucky Charms and coffee for breakfast.

I had a wonderful time that November day, even when I was sitting on that frigid boulder: I had clipped to the back of my belt an orange pad filled with pellets that apparently help preserve body warmth as they're compressed. (Here, of course, is a real technological breakthrough: For once heat is being propelled against the human bottom in the woods, instead of the reverse.)

This was the first time in years I had been in the woods in the winter without wearing cross-country skis, and I had forgotten how magnificent the experience is—and how different it is from tromping around the small forests of Vermont in the summer or fall. I was astonished at the visibility, and the vistas that opened up without any leaves on the trees. It was also a treat to see so clearly the different animal tracks in the snow: a snowshoe hare, a buck, a doe.

Now I know some of you are wondering why a very public vegetarian was in the woods with a gun—albeit one without bullets. A big reason was that a character in a novel I'm writing is a hunter. But I was also hunting—pretending to hunt, really—because I had never done it before and hunting is an important part of Vermont's cultural self-image.

I did not, to be honest, have any overwhelming desire to field-dress a buck, but I did read a manual beforehand about how to do such a thing in the event we actually got a deer. Since Bob was kind enough to take me along, I felt I had a moral obligation to assist him after the kill without vomiting.

Bob and I set off a little before sunrise into the woods high on the mountains here in Lincoln, and by mid-morning I had seen my very first deer beds: two small ovals each the rough size of an automobile tire, the snow melted in the shape of eggs, and the newly exposed oak and maple leaves on the forest floor still warm to the touch. Bob explained that these had been left by a doe and a fawn, and they'd probably been watching us before leaving. A few minutes later we found the tracks where the deer had actually crossed our path—small divots in the snow and the spongy mud, some in the much larger prints from our own boots.

Shortly before lunch we discovered what Bob really was after: the scrapes on the ground left by a buck in full rut, and fresh hooking on the bark of a small tree.

Bob didn't get his deer that day, which meant I didn't need the airsickness bag I had brought with me in the event that he did and we needed to field-dress the animal. The fact is, however, that given the single buck limit, all but one of the days when Bob is in the woods during rifle season he won't get a deer.

And that's fine with him—and with most hunters. Certainly there is the sense of accomplishment and camaraderie that comes with bringing a buck home and watching it get weighed. But hunting, I learned, is as much about a good day in the quiet of the forest as it is about venison.

SNOW COLORS VERMONT IN BEAUTY

ONE PARTICULARLY HOT, humid September day when I was visiting my father in Florida—the sort of day in which Floridians try to remain inside their air-conditioned automobiles and homes, but still wind up drenched in sweat in the few seconds it takes to walk from front door to car door—I asked him why any-one would choose to live in a place where the temperature flirted with triple-digits as late as the first day of fall.

"I wonder the same thing about you folks in Vermont come mid-December," he answered.

Touché. I know I pine for sweat on those brisk winter days when the temperature's hovering between negative digits and insanity, and I know I'll find myself yearning for anyplace warm come early February.

Yet I don't feel that way right now. The first real snow we had this year in Lincoln happened to come at night, but by the next morning the clouds had rolled east. The result? Light was pour-ing in through my bedroom windows as early as 4:45, filling the room with the sort of radiance and luster we usually expect in those months when the days last forever: The room had the glow of June or July.

It was sixteen degrees when I went outside, but there was absolutely no wind, so if it wasn't exactly sweater weather, nor was it call-of-the-wild, leave-no-flesh-exposed cold.

And everything, of course, was white. We tend to modify fresh snow with words like *clean* and *pure,* and certainly they're apt. But rural Vermont in those first hours after a snowstorm is more than clean and pure, it's the sort of vast, trance-like world that fills fairy tales and dreams. Things move more slowly in snow—animals as well as cars—and the world grows quiet. Almost supernaturally quiet.

When I stand outside at 5:00 in the morning in June, at the very least I will hear birds—robins and cardinals and phoebes—and I'll probably hear the squirrels bending the smaller branches of the maples by the barn as they whirl among them like Berbers.

When I stand outside at 5:00 in the morning in December, I

won't hear a thing. It's not quite so cold yet that the trees or houses will snap, and so the world will seem soundless.

And those trees that serve as playgrounds for squirrels in the summer? The first morning after a snow, they become elegant black and crystal sculptures: a willowy raven frame, layered with luminous sky-blown glass. That glass may melt before nine in the morning, but it's still beautiful in the hours it's new.

The main road out of Lincoln in winter winds along the New Haven River, and driving along it immediately after a snowstorm is a wondrous three-and-a-half-mile excursion into a forest that seems genuinely enchanted: The trees form a silvery canopy along much of the road, the boughs bending beneath the weight of the ice and snow like frosted palm fronds.

And even those parts of the world that seem downright prosaic in summer grow mystic in snow. My daughter's swing set becomes albino white in the winter because the snow drapes the blue seats and yellow slide like folded hand towels and quilts. Her sandbox, shaped like a turtle with a shell for a cover, becomes a small igloo. And the patch of earth that had been the vegetable garden—a part of the yard that without snow this time of the year is a depressing brown square dotted with stalks from dead plants and the weeds that just wouldn't die—becomes an elegant stretch of snow-covered beach, with tiny hillocks of chalk and what might be frozen foam rolling ashore from the surf.

I might wonder why we live where we live in another two months, but I don't at this point in December. The first snows are merely a gentle reminder that beauty in Vermont isn't limited to the summer and fall. Splendor here comes in all seasons. Even winter.

CHEATING DEATH IN THE AP-GAP

WE'RE APPROACHING that time of year when the only mammals using the Lincoln Gap to cross between Lincoln and Warren are bears, deer, and people from southern climates who don't comprehend the significance of a sign that says, "Road Not Maintained in Winter."

If the Gap is not closed by now for the season, it soon will be. This means the only way across the mountain is the McCullough Turnpike, or the state's illustrious Vermont 17.

Given the good number of folks in Addison County who commute to work in Montpelier, Waterbury, and the ski resorts lining the eastern slopes of the mountain, Vermont 17 is a busy road in winter.

It is also, however, a scary one. The McCullough Turnpike twists tortuously between Bristol and Waitsfield, with roughly eight miles of stomach-turning switchbacks in its center that rise with serpentine splendor to the top of the Appalachian Gap. Without wanting to belabor the obvious of a road carved into a mountain, the turnpike's distinguishing feature is that it is a steep drive up one hill followed by a steep drive down another.

Yet I have a good many friends who work on the other side of the mountain, and thus traverse the Gap twice a day in the sorts of nasty weather that once excited the producers of *Rescue 911*.

Bristol's Nancy Luke is one. Nancy is the director of adult ski programs at Sugarbush, as well as a ski instructor. She drives daily on what has come to be called the Ap-Gap. Moreover, as a skier—someone who derives pleasure from sliding quickly down hills—she is the perfect sort of person to take on the Ap-Gap without fear or pause or a large insurance policy.

Only once has Nancy failed to conquer the McCullough, and that was when the sand truck before her slid off the road at the summit. She was on her way to work, which meant she was just west of the peak.

Both lanes of the road before her were quilted under so much snow they were impassable, and only her lane was plowed behind her: The other half of the road was still buried, which meant there wasn't even room to turn her car around.

Her solution? "I backed down," she says with a shrug, humbly downplaying the world-class driving accomplishment of all time.

Lincoln's Bill Norton and Larry Masterson are not skiers, but given the way they drive they could be. The two mild-mannered accountants have commuted to Montpelier together for three decades. Since 1976, they've been part of a group who scale the mountain in a—Dramamine, please—van.

Before the van, however, they were part of a foursome who often used Bill's Chevy Nova. Driving a Chevy Nova over a mountain in winter is like sailing Kon-Tiki across the Pacific: a gesture that is intrepid, heroic, and dumb.

Bill says the small group had a little trick to get the Nova over the mountain when the road was covered with ice or snow. Three of the adult men would sit in the trunk to weigh down the rear, while the fourth drove. To report this maneuver with scrupulous accuracy, I should note that Larry—an especially tall man— would actually sit on the edge of the trunk with only his legs inside it.

Almost always this method succeeded, even that morning

when from his perch outside the car Larry saw the sand truck backing down the hill in the Nova's lane before Bill, but despite his frantic banging on the car's roof was unable to get Bill's attention.

At the last minute Bill was able to swerve around the truck, riding one of the snowbanks like a bobsled driver in hot pursuit of a gold.

All the group got to work on time, except Bill.

"It was my car and I was driving," he says, "so I thought I should be the one to clean up the trunk where the guys had been sitting."

SUGARERS SIGNAL END OF WINTER

IT'S A SATURDAY morning in February, and while the sun will soon be high overhead, the temperature's not going to climb above twenty today. It probably won't reach fifteen.

Still, it's a wonderful day to be deep in the woods: Mount Abraham is a giant white snowball against a fluorescent blue sky, and the snow's so fresh you can see the tracks of wild turkeys and moose stretching well into the trees.

Five days a week, Don Gale and Evan Truchon are engineers who spend their days with computers. Today they are sugarmakers. Evan is knee-deep in snow, and Don would be, too, if it weren't for the fifty-year-old snowshoes he's strapped under his boots.

They're stomping high up one of the foothills in the National Forest that rings the western slope of Mount Ellen, attaching plastic tubing to maple trees. They've been hanging that tubing every weekend since the first of the year, and they will probably be back every weekend until the sap starts running in March.

This year they've draped about five thousand new feet of tubing, bringing their total to somewhere between three and four miles. This isn't a huge amount, but it's not shabby. As Truchon observes, "I wouldn't call our sugaring a job because our hourly rate's about a penny. But it takes a lot more work than any hobby I've ever had."

Yet, like most of the state's 2,500 sugarmakers, Truchon and Gale are addicted. And while the part of the process most non-sugarmakers see—those spring days inside a sugarhouse that steams like a sauna and smells like a pure maple spa—is the part we tend to romanticize, these days in the snow and the cold of February are the ones Truchon and Gale like best.

"We can be up here a whole day and not see another human being," Gale says. "And some days it's absolutely quiet: You don't hear a sound but the crunching of the snow as you break a trail."

Today, however, they do have company (other than me) and there is noise. A woodpecker is trailing them, pausing always two or three trees from the maple they're looping with the small links of hose they call "drops." When the temperature warms, they will tap these maples, inserting a spout from the drop into the tree.

And while they rarely see other people up here, they do see animals. Wild turkeys are common, and so are deer. Occasionally they see moose, including one early this year that Truchon watched lumber up to one of their lines, raise it with her nose, and then stroll underneath it.

The one constant is the work: It's always hard. Forty pounds of tubing might not sound like a lot, but it grows heavy fast when you're climbing uphill, your feet sinking two and three feet into the snow. And then, when the pair arrive at a tree to attach one of the drops, they need to peel off the flaps of their hunting gloves—gloves in which the fingers extend only as far as the first knuckle, but have a special fold-over mitten—and expose their fingers to the cold. It's no easy task to link two pieces of plastic tubing in sub-freezing weather, and they depend upon a thermos of hot water to make the lines malleable.

Yet the two men relish this time. It may simply be that the labor is profoundly different from their work designing electrical boards or machines that grind marble: It is certainly not sedentary, and no part of it demands a keyboard and a monitor.

But it might be more than that. It might also be the opportunity to get outside while there's still snow and silence in the woods, and no leaves to canopy the trail from the sun. Soon the snow will be gone, and while these woods may not be densely aboriginal, they are deep and quiet and a pretty good stretch from a world of snowmobiles and skis.

Here is not a bad place at all to savor the end of the season.

SELECT NUMBERS SHOW A CHANGING VERMONT

THREE WEEKS AGO I found the lid to my septic tank without having to avail myself of my neighbor Rudy Cram's wisdom.

Usually the only way I find my septic tank lid is by digging for nine solid hours, having my wife flush a toilet seven hundred times inside while I lie on the ground outside with my ear pressed to the grass, and then—when all else has failed—asking Rudy if he knows where the septic tank is.

When it comes to houses, especially mine, Rudy knows everything.

This year, however, I actually found the septic tank myself. I didn't even need to wander around my yard like a somnambulant madman with a dowsing rod in my hands.

I was very proud, and when I boasted of this monumental accomplishment to my wife, she observed that my newly found competency might have something to do with the reality that we've now lived in Lincoln for a decade and a half.

Tuesday, as a matter of fact, marks our fifteen-year anniversary in this house in Vermont.

In that period there have been enormous changes in our fair state, of which my ability to find my septic tank is only one. Depending upon whether one wants a VCR or a view, Taft Corners has metamorphosed from a cow pasture into either a convenient shopping mecca or a sprawl of cement bunkers.

The Queen City's iconoclastic firebrand of a mayor has become the Green Mountains' somewhat more inhibited but no less independent congressman. And our legislative language is now peppered with wondrously provocative terms that meant nothing in the mid-1980s, including, of course, civil union.

There have been a variety of more subtle changes, however, that in their own way are no less telling and bear testimony to the state's transformation. To wit:

- In 1986, there were exactly six traffic lights in the thirty-two miles separating my home and this newspaper's newsroom in downtown Burlington; today there are nineteen.

- Fifteen years ago, the state issued 91,039 hunting licenses to residents; last year it issued 83,593.

- The deer herd numbered roughly 110,000 in 1986; today it's closer to 145,000.

- Number of Wal-Marts in Vermont in 1986: zero. Number today: four.

- Fifteen years ago, there were a mere 1,267 Vermont-licensed attorneys in the state; today there are 2,688.

- The state boasted 3,044 dairy farms in 1986; today there are 1,565.

- Numbers are less exact for emu farms. In 1986 in Vermont there was either one emu farm or zero; today there are nine or ten.

- Fifteen years ago, there were 8,267 serious crimes in Chittenden County; by last year the total had fallen to 6,630.

- In 1986, Vermont Public Radio had two stations and 32,000 listeners; today there are five stations and 160,000 listeners.

- If you wanted a cup of coffee in downtown Burlington in 1986, you were likely to drop into places like the Oasis, Henry's Diner, or the Woolworth on Church Street. Now you're likely to visit Muddy Waters, Uncommon Grounds, Starbucks, or Speeder & Earl's.

- There were approximately 310 country stores in the Green Mountains in 1986; today there are 210. And while the number of grocery stores has decreased as well, falling from eighty to sixty, the newer ones are twice as large as the older ones.

- Number of snowmobiles registered with the Department of Motor Vehicles in 1986: 29,705. Number today: 36,077.

And, of course, the number of hours it has taken me to find my septic tank has plummeted from nine to a fraction of one. This, in my mind, is an incontrovertible sign of progress.

THE CHURCH
WITH A
WEATHERVANE
ATOP THE STEEPLE

A FENDER BENDER WITH BABY JESUS?

I HAVE MANY FEARS, some more rational than others, but one is about to go away for a little while because Christmas is coming.

For the next few weeks, I will no longer fear running over the baby Jesus in his creche.

This is actually one of my more rational fears.

Specifically, I fear that some day between mid-January and mid-December, I might have to pull myself together after a tremendous calamity has occurred for which I am responsible, and struggle over to the United Church of Lincoln and explain to the congregation, "Ummm, there's no good way to say this, but I think I just ran over the baby Jesus. I'm really sorry, but I accidentally put the car into drive instead of reverse, and you know the incredible pickup those Plymouth Colts have."

This could happen. This could happen because my church's almost life-size nativity scene is stored inside my barn after Christmas, and it is stored about a foot from the front bumper of my car after I've parked.

Add to this the fact that I am an incredibly incompetent driver, and some days I am getting into my car at six in the morning— a time of day when I'm an even worse driver than usual, because I haven't yet hooked up the intravenous caffeine feed that keeps me awake—and we have a prescription for disaster.

Ironically, it was my lamebrained idea to put the creche where it is in the first place. About five years ago, the stewards asked if the church could store the nativity scene in my barn instead of my neighbor's, where it had sat for years. I knew this nativity scene well, I knew the faces of the folks in the manger, and they seemed like nice enough people. So I said sure, they could summer in my barn.

What I didn't know was that the nativity scene weighed a little more than a backhoe. This isn't one of those particleboard nativity scenes, this is no spit-and-polish plastic affair. This is a nativity scene with a five-foot-high manger, wooden adults who have eaten well for most of their wooden lives, and a floor with an aircraft carrier hidden inside it to keep the thing stable when the December winds blow hard off the mountain.

It takes six strong men to carry it the fifty yards from the church to my barn.

For four years we put the creche in the back of the barn, on the wooden floor far from the car. Over time, however, the flooring began to sink under its weight, and the wall beside it started to sag accordingly.

So this past January, I suggested we put the manger on the edge of the cement pad in the front half of the barn, where I park. There is just enough room in this garage bay for the nativity scene, the car, and one thin person to stand.

Consequently, when I drive into the barn at night, my headlights beam the creche. When I start the car in the morning, there are three shepherds, Mary and Joseph, and the baby Jesus staring back at me from the manger.

This is a very weird sensation: bumper-to-bumper with the baby Jesus.

It is also, however, an extremely moving one. In addition to the symbolic meaning of the creche to Christians worldwide, this particular creche has additional meaning to the members of one small church in Lincoln.

No one knows who built it. It appeared, mysteriously, on Christmas Eve, 1981, on the lawn of the church the year the church had burned to the ground. When I see the creche, I am therefore reminded that while one old church may have disappeared in smoke and flame, in its ashes was faith, and from that faith a new church arose.

So in three weeks, when it's time to move the creche back into the barn after Christmas, I probably won't find a new spot. But I will learn to drive with the parking brake on.

CLOUDS CAN'T HIDE THE SUN
ON A SPIRITUALLY BRIGHT
EASTER MORNING

MOUNT ABRAHAM HAS no Himalayan aspirations, no delusions that it is part of a particularly grand massif. Just above four thousand feet, it is among the taller mountains in Vermont, but it is still less than one-seventh the height of Everest.

Nevertheless, it towers above the village of Lincoln, its summit just east of the town, and offers a remarkably different visage when scrutinized from different angles.

Peter and Sue Brown, for example, who live to the southwest in a farmhouse Robert Frost once tried to buy, see what has always looked to me like a gargantuan toppled pear. John Nelson and Christine Fraioli, who live due west of the mountain, see instead a more gently sloping incline: A colossal bunny hill for a giant just learning to ski.

It is not uncommon for there to be a layer of clouds just below the summit but nothing but clear sky above 3,500 feet. When this happens, the peak can look a bit like a boulder at the seashore at low tide: The clouds become sea foam and the mountaintop—white in the winter, brown in the spring, a deep green in the long days of summer—grows reminiscent of a stone in the breakers.

When this occurs in the very early morning, before the sun has come fully over the top, the clouds become an almost nuclear shade of orangy red.

One of the best views of the mountain is from Gove Hill, a gentle knoll south of the center of the village that is bordered by woods to the west. The hill is just steep enough that in the winter children can race down it on their snowboards and sleds.

This morning, Easter, a good number of us from churches in Lincoln and Bristol will gather on that hill and watch the mountain to the east. We will arrive there before 6:00 A.M., and we will hope that today will be one of those sunrises in which we do indeed see the great star slowly emerge over Abraham. We do this every year, a ritual we share with congregations all over the world.

One of the great idiosyncracies of the sunrise service on Gove Hill, however, is that we never know what to expect in terms of the weather. This is Vermont, after all, and Easter falls in that time of the year when the climate can only be called capricious. In recent years, the small congregation has gathered in the midst of howling snowstorms, and on balmy spring days when the daffodils and crocuses have already pushed through the boggy ground—kaleidoscopically beautiful signs of rebirth.

There have been many Easters when the mountain has been completely obscured by fog and clouds, and the only evidence we've had that the sun is up is that the asphalt-gray sky has grown marginally lighter.

At the same time, there have been Easters when the clouds have been a pure white woolpack just below the summit, with the sky above them a cerulean blue. Those mornings we have sung a hymn, and the sun has appeared miraculously over the mountain—seemingly at the same height as our little perch on Gove Hill. Those moments are a particular blessing.

But gather we do, regardless of whether we need to tromp up the hill in our mud boots and parkas or in light sweaters and sneakers. Sometimes there are fifty of us, sometimes there are a hundred. But the size of the congregation is less relevant, it seems, than the fact we are a part of a fellowship. We have been taught, after all, that it takes only a few of us to gather for there to be a church.

Likewise, the unpredictability of the vista before us and the fact the sun and the mountain may be obscured are gentle reminders of just how little we know and how much we must take on faith. The sun will rise, we believe, regardless of whether we see it.

Happy Easter. Happy Passover. Peace.

FAITH GIVES A CHILD SERENITY

MY WIFE, my three-year-old daughter, and I are sitting around the kitchen counter where we have breakfast and lunch most weekends. It's just after noon on a Sunday.

With the pensiveness that is peculiar to small children—my daughter's lips are drawn tight and her chin is tilted down toward her chest, but her eyes are looking up without a trace of a pout—she asks almost abruptly, "God's really strong, right?"

"Certainly," I answer, and then quickly translate my response into one of the colloquialisms she hears around the house all the time: "Sure is."

And although I'm not surprised that God is on her mind—she has, after all, just returned from Sunday school—I inquire as casually as I can, "So, why do you ask?"

"Welllll," she says, drawing the word out the way she does whenever she's figuring something out. "Your mommy died. And mommy's daddy died. And God had to carry them both up to heaven."

I nod, desperately in love with both her logic and her faith. (Meanwhile, the literalist inside me I've never liked much is thinking, "Well, they died four years apart, Grace, so God didn't have to carry them up to heaven at exactly the same time. There were probably two trips." Fortunately, I keep my mouth shut.)

"Yeah, I thought so," she murmurs, and then contentedly takes another bite of her cheese sandwich, moving on blithely to the next question in her head: whether her mother and I will allow her to inebriate the cat with catnip that afternoon.

I pray that my daughter never loses her faith. I pray that children of every faith retain their assurance that there's more in this world than they can see and comprehend, and that their confidence always remains a part of who they are.

Some days, of course, that prayer seems more reasonable than others. I've certainly sat through funerals in which my own faith was challenged: the funerals of friends who in my mind died way too young. Sometimes I marvel that faith even survives in a world that in recent history has offered us ethnic cleansing in what was once Yugoslavia, mass slaughter in Rwanda, and people willing to blow up whole buildings in Oklahoma, Argentina, and Dhahran.

I have an older friend who attended divinity school with every intention of becoming a clergyman. But he found that in his case, the more he studied, the more his faith diminished. Eventually he dropped out and went on to a successful career in market research. In his life's work, the thorny issue of blind faith was made irrelevant by focusing instead on those questions and problems that lent themselves to statistical analysis and concrete projections.

And there's no doubt in my mind that faith is capricious. My mother-in-law is an unwavering atheist, while her brother was for decades an Episcopal minister who works now for the Episcopal diocese in Chicago.

But faith is also accessible. It's a gift given to the soul the moment we begin to sense the mysteries that surround us: an absolute intangible such as love. Those small and large acts of seemingly unreasonable selflessness that pepper our days and our nights. The astonishing goodness and beneficence that bob like buoys in the maelstrom that is this planet so much of the time.

There's something miraculous in the very premise of spring.

And faith is a boon that seems always there for the taking. Sometimes it demands a little work: a participation in the rituals the soul is craving. Acquiescing to the likelihood that we don't know quite as much as we thought. A willingness to bow before the notion that for once in our lives we have to swallow our pride and ask for something we need.

But the gift has always struck me as enormous: a whole life lived with the peace of mind of a three-year-old.

MARRIAGE WEDS LOVE TO LAUGHTER

I ALWAYS KNEW the pastor of our church had a pretty good arm from center field, but I'd never realized his biceps were so large until I saw them in a sleeveless white wedding gown.

Likewise, I'd never imagined that construction manager Mike Stone could make a Barney-purple cocktail dress and high heels work so well with his mustache and goatee, or that Wendy Truax and Helen Turner could don men's suits and produce a fashion statement that was certainly bold . . . but at least not completely insane.

And I'd certainly never realized accordion music needn't always be a crime: There is only magic in the way Libby Atkins plays her half-century-old Sereni, a joy in her "Blue Barrel Polka."

Frankly, there may be no better way to savor those last warm Saturday afternoons in Vermont than to attend an outdoor wedding re-enactment, with the sun still high and hot at midday, the gathering at once ebullient and restrained, and the large bridal party completely in drag.

Clearly, there are thousands of reasons why I cherish Vermont (and even more when I think specifically of Lincoln), but Mike's and Wendy's willingness to wear purple silk and gray flannel respectively to help four friends celebrate two wedding anniversaries must be among them.

Twenty-five years ago, the twin Goodyear girls of Lincoln, Lorraine and Lenore, were married in one ceremony to Bob Patterson and Russ Gates. Their double marriage was recently reenacted in Lincoln at a surprise silver anniversary party for the two couples, and well over 150 friends and family members descended upon the center of town to toast the Pattersons and the Gateses and witness the incredible simulation.

The identical twin brides were played by identical twins David and Paul Wood, and the grooms were played by the Pattersons' and the Gateses' teenage daughters, Krista and Alison.

Sociologists or psychologists or cultural historians could probably read into that mock wedding—and the rural tradition of which it's a part—whatever they wanted. There's a lot there, the ritual is layered with meanings: the roles of women and men, the power of costume and dress, the simple fact that the days get too short too fast in this part of the globe.

Arguably, the greatest fashion no-no that occurred at the wedding—the most glaring violation of gender dress norms— probably hung from the shoulders of my friend Wendy Truax: You wouldn't see me wear a gray flannel suit when the temperature's still flirting with ninety degrees. You wouldn't see most people (guys or gals) do it.

Yet Wendy did, and she did it for, well, love. Maybe laughs and love. Maybe laughs, love, and the chance to embarrass Lorraine and Lenore. But love was definitely in the equation.

That's what I saw most in that mock ceremony in Lincoln. I saw the deep-rooted affection a great many people have for the Pattersons and the Gateses, and their profound awareness of the myriad ways the four lovers have brought joy to the lives that surround them. I've probably attended a half-dozen weddings in my life in which we were reminded of the apostle Paul's words to the Corinthians—love is patient and kind and endures all things— but it was only in that faux ceremony that I saw Sarah's testimony in Genesis that love is also about laughter.

Today is my twelfth anniversary with my own inamorata: my enchantress, my bride, my wife. If, in thirteen years, we are surprised by a bridal party in drag (my teen daughter as me in a tux, my pastor in white as my wife), I will consider it evidence of a life lived well, in a small world that understands the meaning of ritual, celebration . . . and a guy in chiffon.

THANK YOU, FRIEND, FOR GUIDING
ME DEEPER INTO MY FAITH

"I AM A Christian because of Owen Meany," the fictional John Wheelwright observes in the first sentence of John Irving's wondrous and complex novel, *A Prayer for Owen Meany.* The book is a decade old now, but that sentence comes back to me often, especially when I contemplate the oddly comforting ruination of reason that is my faith.

Most of the time I am not altogether sure why I am a Christian. I'm a confirmed Episcopalian, but much of my study involved listening to *Jesus Christ Superstar* in my older brother's bedroom while rifling through his drawers to see what he was hiding beneath his socks.

Growing up, I went to church on Easter and Christmas, but I have no memories of Sunday school. It wasn't that my parents were particularly remiss. In fact, they weren't remiss at all when it came to most things, and I had a glorious childhood. But this was suburban New York in the 1960s and '70s—a small world of impressively dysfunctional Cheever-esque excess—and my friends and I didn't know it was possible to be an adult on a Sunday morning who was simultaneously awake and not hungover.

Even then, there was something that was drawing me beyond *Star Trek* spirituality. I read often about the Crucifixion, and at age eleven, I could have volunteered the information to anyone who was interested that a Roman nail was about as thick as a Magic Marker, and why the Mediterranean heat made crucifixion an especially gruesome way to die.

Nevertheless, I managed to keep organized religion at a safe distance as a young adult—so distant, in fact, that people who I knew long ago are astonished when we meet now and they discover my faith.

There was one time last fall when I was at a bookstore in Minneapolis and a woman I hadn't seen since 1982 approached me. I showed her the cover of my new novel and pointed out to her the church.

"I'm a deacon there," I said.

Her mouth hung open for what seemed like an hour. I could have counted the fillings in her lower teeth. "You?" she said finally, too astonished to croak out more than a syllable.

Of course, the person she'd known in college was considerably different from the person I am now. Not better or worse. But twenty years ago when someone would approach me with his belief in a God who was knowing and loving and kind, I would usually nod and then ask him to explain Auschwitz to me. Or Bangladesh. Or childhood diseases that take people when they're young.

I still wonder sometimes.

But it no longer diminishes my faith—which is a real shocker for some of my friends. It's as if it is impossible to reconcile rigorous intellectualism with spirituality.

Yet the world is filled with devout Christians and Jews and Muslims who are dramatically more educated than I am, and considerably smarter. I would never question the rightness of anyone's faith—or, equally as important, the meaningfulness of anyone's doubt. We believe what we believe.

Which brings me back to why I am a Christian today. There was no sudden infusion of light, there were no voices inviting me in. There was no near-death experience; there was no collapse into drinking and drugs. My wife and I did buy a house next to a church—which certainly made getting to the sanctuary once a week easier than if we'd actually had to get in a car and drive— but even that isn't why I'm a Christian.

This week, the pastor of that church next to our house, David Wood, celebrates his twentieth year in the pulpit. Two decades at the United Church of Lincoln. We are the only parish he has ever had, and, speaking selfishly, the only one I hope he ever has.

David was among the first people I met in Lincoln, and a fine introduction to the community. But he was also the perfect soul to guide me to that cliff from which one must shed disbelief and shirk gravity. He evidences more patience in a day than I will show in a lifetime, and he is as gentle with people as the best mothers and fathers are with their children. He is knowledgeable, comfortable with doubt, and a great listener—which is no small accomplishment since, as he knows, without his hearing aids he is as deaf as a post.

And so perhaps when I think of why I am what I am, when I deconstruct the different components that comprise the intangibles of my spirit, I can echo John Wheelwright: I am a Christian, at least in part, because of David Wood.

Happy anniversary, friend.

THE
CEMETERY

OF MEMORY AND HOPE

THEY COME WITH dandelions, since dandelions are plentiful in the last week of May and may be picked with impunity. They arrive around 9:30 in the morning, and as they walk underneath the wrought-iron gate that is three and four times their height, they abruptly stop hopping or skipping or trying to step on the heels of the children in front of them.

Suddenly, they are attempting to behave like grown-ups. They disperse into small groups, but they walk slowly among the tombstones and markers, pausing when they see a name that they know, squatting when they discover a relative. The boys stand with their hands clasped before them, replicating the ways they've seen their fathers and grandfathers stand, while the girls sometimes hold hands.

Every year on the first school day after Memorial Day, the children of the elementary school in Lincoln, Vermont, walk about a mile from the red cedar building that houses the school to the village cemetery. The school is east of the center of town, and the cemetery is to the west.

The result is a rambling parade through the village: 106 students, kindergartners through sixth-graders, fourteen teachers and administrators, and perhaps a dozen members of the support staff. They walk across the narrow bridge spanning the New Haven River and then past the line of Gothic Revival homes built a century and a half ago. They pass the gray clapboard general store and the town hall with its imposing brick walls and slate roof. Then they wander around the hill upon which sits a church built in 1863, and down the short street that once housed the village's modest creamery. They walk right past my house. And, all along the way, they stop, bend down, and pluck the dandelions they will use to decorate the graves, many of which will have small American flags.

For some of the children, there is a special satisfaction when they find a rusted star on a pole in the ground. Underneath the corrosion on that star are the letters G.A.R., signifying the Grand Army of the Republic. Finding a G.A.R. star is a bit like finding Waldo. It means that someone has found the grave site of a Civil War veteran.

Finding a G.A.R. veteran is not the sole reason they come— that war, after all, is ancient history to them, as unreal as the struggles of Odysseus, Menelaus, and Agamemnon. But it does help explain why Mom and Dad didn't go to work on Monday, and why they themselves haven't gone to school for three days.

Their search does, ironically, bring history to life. After all, Memorial Day, now a three-day festival of barbecues, beach picnics, and golf, has its origins in the carnage of Chickamauga, Antietam, and Petersburg. The idea of taking the holiday at face value and pausing to memorialize or remember the fallen war dead is considered by some to be unstylish at best, militaristic at worst.

Certainly, I, at first, had mixed emotions. I'm a thirty-something kid from the suburbs of New York City who never even considered enlisting when I registered for the draft twenty years ago. The notion that Memorial Day had more meaning than a long weekend was beyond me. But then I moved to Vermont a decade ago, and in Lincoln I learned that Memorial Day is neither anachronistic nor sentimental.

The holiday is still called "Decoration Day" here by the elderly who can remember grandfathers and great-grandfathers who helped quash what Memorial Day founder General John Logan termed the "rebellion." It has metamorphosed into an opportunity to honor all the grandparents and parents and uncles and aunts who have come before us. It doesn't seem to matter whether they served the country as warriors or served the community by plowing the roads in winter.

The kids, more times than not, simply place the dandelions atop the graves of the names they know. And while Decoration Day may have been proposed by a general, it seems appropriate that the long-dormant tradition of visiting the cemetery in Lincoln was resurrected sixteen years ago by Phoebe Barash, a school principal who spent her adolescence at a Quaker boarding school in Pennsylvania and rallied against the Vietnam War while at Wheelock College, in Boston.

A century ago, it wasn't uncommon for Vermont schoolchildren to be taken to the village cemetery to decorate the headstones of veterans with flowers and flags. Dorothy Canfield Fisher, a Vermont author and one of the first members of the Book-of-the-Month Club selection committee, observed the ritual in "Memorial Day," a short story she wrote just before the Second World War:

> Flags lay flat on the wreaths of flowers held by the little country boys who filled the car to the brim. When it stopped at the gate of the cemetery, the little boys spilled themselves out. Like the grass and trees and other growing things, they were quivering and glistening with vital-

ity. Their small bodies were clad in their Sunday clothes, their hair was smoothly brushed back from their round, well-soaped faces. Everyone wore a necktie. Everyone carried on his arm a wreath to decorate a soldier's grave.

The irony of Fisher's tale is that while it's clear the author appreciated the pomp attending the cemetery visit, the story offers a decidedly antiwar message. As the boys fantasize about the heroism of the men beneath the ground, glamorizing their deaths, the ghosts of the dead soldiers are screaming silently for them to go away, wishing desperately that the living could hear them. The presence of the children has awakened them from their sleep, and once more they are feeling the bullets and bayonets that killed them.

Barash—like Fisher, like me—once had a decidedly love-hate relationship with the holiday. On the one hand, Barash recalls, when she decided to resurrect the tradition in Lincoln, she wanted to be sure that she wasn't deifying battle; on the other hand, she wanted the kids in her charge to have a sense of history. "Children who went to elementary school in the 1970s missed out on the part of our heritage we call patriotism," Barash explains, "and so bringing back the visit to the cemetery was a way to give them a taste of it. It was an opportunity to honor people who've come before us."

No one is sure exactly why or when the Lincoln school stopped decorating the graves on Memorial Day. In all likelihood, it was simply logistics: Today, Lincoln has a single large, centrally located school, but at one point, the 1,063-person community had five tiny ones spread out among 26,000 acres of dairy farms, woods, and dirt roads. Pure and simple, most of those schools were too far away to have the children walk to the graveyard.

Might other Vermont communities have given up on the ritual for a similar reason? Perhaps. Some may have grown too large for the practice, while others may have grown too small. In some towns, the fathers and mothers and teachers who would have had to coordinate the tradition may have grown indifferent once the last surviving Civil War veterans died.

Or maybe the tradition simply faded when the adults discovered they could have a parade instead. Parades, after all, are considerably less morbid than a visit to a graveyard, especially if you muster the local firefighters in their trucks and put a few aged veterans in convertibles.

Today, as many as a quarter of Vermont's 251 towns may have a Memorial Day ceremony or parade, but no more than a handful have an organized school visit to the cemetery.

Clearly, however, the Lincoln children do not find their excursion to the cemetery frightening. Nor do they find the rite hollow. Alice Leeds, a fifth- and sixth-grade teacher at the school, has noticed that once the children have found their share of G.A.R. stars and American flags, they begin what is for them the real work at hand: They visit their family plots. Sometimes that means running their fingers over the name of a distant aunt or a grandfather they barely knew. But sometimes it means something more.

In the case of Rebecca Wedge, now fourteen, it meant visiting the spot where her father was buried. Leeds will always remember the way Wedge's friends had wrapped their arms around the young girl as they approached the grave site. Likewise, Leeds will never forget the way Matthew Miller's friends had stood like an honor guard before Matt's father's plot. "It's more about ancestry than warfare," Leeds says of the school's tradition. "For the kids, it's one more way of discovering their connection to their community."

Building contractor Terry Farr and his dog, a golden retriever that he calls The Boss, will wander up and down the rows of Lincoln's Maple Cemetery this Saturday, looking for veterans' graves. Whenever Terry finds one, he will stick a small nylon flag into the ground beside the tombstone.

Farr, forty, is a member of the Sons of the American Legion, a group that includes anyone who is not himself a veteran but is a direct descendant of one. (Farr's grandfather fought in the First World War.) The Bristol Post of the Sons of the American Legion takes responsibility for decorating the cemeteries for Memorial Day in Bristol and the surrounding communities, which includes Lincoln.

It will take Farr a little more than two hours to comb the Lincoln cemetery. Altogether, he will find the graves of close to 150 veterans, including 101 from the Civil War. But he will also find five from the Revolutionary War, two of whose names still resonate in Lincoln: Briggs (on a hill) and Burnham (on the town hall). There are veterans in the cemetery who fought in the War of 1812, the First and Second World Wars, the Korean War, and in Southeast Asia.

Douglas Gordon Orvis, a first lieutenant in an air cavalry division, was twenty-six when the patrol he was leading in July 1968 was ambushed in Vietnam, and he was killed. His marker is one of the most visited in the cemetery, because engraved on a plaque on a rock beside it is part of a letter he penned when he was only twenty-one: "There is something infinitely strong in a mountain. If only a man could mold and nourish something of it within himself." From his plot, there is a magnificent view of Mount Abraham, the giant toppled peach of a mountain that towers over the village of Lincoln.

What seems to matter to the children, however, is less the notion that Douglas Orvis may have been a hero than the fact that he was an Orvis—a common name in the town and a link between the present and the past. Once I listened to a group of older elementary school kids as they stood by his plot, and the focus of their conversation was not upon the war but upon his family. Everyone knew someone who was related to Douglas.

Once the children have had a chance to roam the cemetery, they gather near the flagpole west of the entrance, where a member of the Bristol band plays taps on a cornet and the Rev. David Wood, the pastor of the local church, speaks briefly about the meaning of the holiday.

For him, Wood says, the meaning of the day has changed over the years. While there will always be a certain wistfulness to any genuine Memorial Day commemoration, Wood believes that "the holiday is as much about life as it is about death. It's a way of celebrating the life of anyone who has come before us, regardless of whether they were in the military."

Indeed, on a morning at the very end of May, when the sun is high and the sky is cerulean—when the grass is neon green and the dandelions are brighter than lemons—one can't help but look to the future with hope. This may be a holiday that began with the request that we stand beside graves and remember the dead, but when those graves are surrounded by children, it's impossible not to focus on the living as well, and to leave the cemetery with a smile.

A PASSING OF HISTORY AND
HOSPITALITY

THE FLOWERS WERE yellow and white along the southern tip of Marshall Hutchins's casket (lilies and daisies), and pink and blue toward the north (delphinia, larkspur, and roses). This wasn't the result of anyone's design or chosen aesthetic, it was simply the way the flowers had arrived.

Marshall's funeral began just after lunch on an overcast Monday toward the end of September, but the clouds were drifting east throughout the service. By the time the choir stood to sing "How Great Thou Art" toward the end, sunlight was sluicing through the thin tunnels of stained glass along the sanctuary wall: forty-five-degree angles of light, each an ethereal buttress that seemed to support the structure, but was, in reality, sustaining Marshall's family and friends.

Marshall Hutchins was seventy-eight when he died, and we were only acquaintances. To imply we were more would be unfair to his memory.

But the paths of our lives crossed once, and they met at the clearing in which I now sit. And type. And remember.

I am writing in the room that was the bedroom Marshall shared with his wife, Louise. A room away—across an entry hall and a stairway—my daughter's troll house rests on the spot where Marshall's easy chair once sat.

Upstairs, I hear my wife at work in the room in which I discovered my two favorite antique newspaper clippings. One marks the perfect game that New York Yankees pitcher Don Larsen hurled in the 1956 World Series (an achievement that is remarkable not because it was in the World Series, but because Larsen was an unremarkable pitcher at best). The other is a front page story from the newspaper describing the incredible possibility that Montpelier and Burlington might someday be linked by a four-lane "super highway."

Those newspapers were laid on the floor underneath a linoleum rug that Marshall—perhaps Marshall and his then young son, Roy, or Marshall and his brother Martyn—had laid.

I live in the yellow house in Lincoln that for almost four decades belonged to Marshall and Louise. I've lived here ten years now (ten years, in fact, this month), but to this day when I meet elderly people for the first time in the nearby supermarket, they are likely to nod and say, "Oh, yes. You live in Marshall's house, don't you?"

I do indeed, and I am glad. Marshall and I first met in the summer of 1986. I was a young, presumptuous New Yorker in a gray suit. He was an older, wiser retired state legislator, selectperson, and volunteer firefighter.

Marshall was not the sort who would ever have pointed out to me the tremendous amount that—to paraphrase Disney's Pocahontas—I didn't even know I didn't know.

Instead, when it was clear that my wife and I were buying his house, he phoned the cubbyhole I was renting in Burlington one September evening and asked, "You lived in New York, right?"

"Right."

He then extended to me one of the most important invitations I've ever received in my life: "Want to come down here Saturday? Have a glass of cider and some doughnuts? This house runs pretty good, but there are a few things I can show you."

I don't know if my wife and I would have survived our first winter here without that autumn Saturday. I still have the yellow legal pad filled with my notes about the furnace and the kitchen heater, the water tank and the fuse box. I still have memories of those doughnuts, my first in the fall in Vermont.

And I still have—and will probably have always—the sense, thanks to Marshall, that houses have histories. Sharing his with me was not merely a pro forma part of the process of selling a house.

It was a ritual of transition. A gesture of hospitality. It was his way of welcoming me to Lincoln.

AN ELEGY FOR THE STATE'S FINEST RED SOX FAN

VERMONT'S—PERHAPS New England's—greatest Red Sox fan died the other day.

He died at the age of eighty-one, as peacefully as anyone can who has watched an endless litany of pennants and titles and world championships slip away.

His name was Ken Hallock, a farmer from Waltham who lived the last fifteen years of his life up in Lincoln. He was certainly not the most famous Red Sox supporter, nor was he the most articulate when it came to that special, heartbreaking kind of masochism that links the fans to the team. You won't, for example, find his poems about Fenway Park in collections with Donald Hall, nor will you find his essays about the game reprinted with those of Bart Giamatti or George Will.

But he was aware without question that to root for the Red Sox—to root with knowledge and passion and patience—is to root as an act of faith. It is to love people who you know will disappoint you, but to forgive them and to love them just the same.

It is to know people are human.

I met Ken Hallock when I sat behind him in church. My wife and I had arrived in Lincoln only three days earlier, and she steered us to the pew behind the "nice older couple" who had brought her a Christmas cactus our first day in town. He spoke to me at the end of the service, after the minister had given the benediction. Taking my hand and shaking it vigorously, he exclaimed, "God loves you, and so do I!"

The jaded New Yorker in me said—for lack of anything better—"Thank you." But I was nonetheless touched and flattered to be accepted without judgment by both him and his God.

When I learned from Mr. Hallock that he was a Red Sox fan, I wasn't at all surprised—not because he was a native New Englander, but because of his confidence that the meek someday will indeed inherit the earth. I only knew Mr. Hallock from church, and I only knew him in the context of church, but I believe the same optimism that served as the foundation for his faith in God, served also to buoy him through the hard times with the Red Sox.

I know, for example, that every year he would make a pilgrimage down country to watch the team play, and almost every time it lost. Sometimes in the last inning.

I know that although he listened religiously to their games on the radio, it was not uncommon for the reception to disappear. Usually in the midst of a rally.

And I know how well he handled what had to have been the most astonishing Red Sox collapse of his life: the 1986 World Series loss to the New York Mets. He was undaunted. He was completely undaunted, even though the team managed to let its first title in almost seventy years slip away when it was only one out from victory. One out! A cluster of bloop singles and a ninety-foot squibber was all it took to dash the team's—and Mr. Hallock's—dreams of a championship.

From the pew behind him, I witnessed Mr. Hallock bear this defeat with his customary courage. The Sunday after the Red Sox had lost he turned to me and said, "As awful as that was, it'll only make next year even sweeter when they win!" And if I had any doubts about the sincerity of his faith, they were dispelled by the way he sang our last hymn, raising his arms and uttering and repeating the words, "How great Thou art, how great Thou art."

Ken Hallock was buried in a small family plot in Waltham, wearing the Red Sox warm-up jacket that helped him to remember that no cause, not even the Red Sox, is so irrevocably lost as to be beyond hope.

HOW A FAMILY COPES WITH LOSS: BUILDING LOVE ON LITTLE WHITE LIES

THE WORLD IS rich with elegies for mothers, so I will spare you one more. Besides, my mother was never particularly good with good-byes ("See you," with a small salute was about as good as it got), and I believe she would prefer that the idiosyncratic privacies of our parting and her death were preserved.

But amidst those moments last month, her last in this world, was one that will endure for me as both a wondrous illustration of the love my family shares, and the weird ways our little clan functions. Or malfunctions. Or—to take grammatical license with an especially popular little adjective—dysfunctions.

On July 5, my father was flat on his back in a Florida hospital, awaiting an angioplasty. My mother was home alone with her cough, hoping desperately that the hack was the result of radiation, pneumonia, or a virus that had besieged her body after months of chemotherapy.

At that point she had been battling lung cancer for eight months, and she still clung to the dream—evaporating a bit with each rasp—that she was getting better.

My mother's oncologist was making his rounds at the hospital that morning and saw my father. He shared with him some bad news: The X-rays he'd taken of my mother's lungs the previous week showed, to use his words, "a significant infiltration."

He wouldn't know for sure until a CAT-scan was done, but the prognosis was bleak.

My father had been an extraordinary cancer coach: part dietitian, part nurse, part-Knute Rockne. The day after my mother had been told of her cancer, he'd bought a Vita-Mix blender for broccoli shakes and carrot juice. When my mother decided she'd prefer not to wear wigs, he bought her hats and scarves and turbans with the care he had once reserved for blouses and jewelry on her birthday.

He called me from his hospital bed with the news, unwilling to share it with my mother on the phone, but unable to keep it solely to himself. The doctor had said he would tell my mother some version of the truth that afternoon when he was scheduled to see her in his office to discuss the X-rays. He had added that he would be gentle, possibly evasive, and my father needn't fear my mother would get the worst of the news while he was unable to comfort her.

My brother and I agreed we would leave for Florida: He'd leave immediately from New York, and I'd fly down the next day.

My father's angioplasty was not scheduled until the evening, and so he called again that afternoon. He sounded tired but peculiarly happy: He must have misunderstood the oncologist that morning, he said. My mother had just told him of her meeting with the doctor, and while there was a spot on the X-ray, it might be just a pneumonia scar. They'd do a CAT-scan to be sure, but we needn't despair just yet. More important, he said, I had to get a message to my brother, who was 35,000 feet off the ground, and tell him that he should not convey to our mother our fear that her time might be short.

I said I would. I was surprised my mother's doctor had painted so rosy a picture, but I assumed he knew what he was doing.

My father had the angioplasty that night, and by July 6, we were together as a family. We all took comfort in the idea there was still room for hope, and I know at least twice I said something to my mother about "that pneumonia scar in your lungs."

I didn't believe for one moment it was a pneumonia scar, but I did believe this was what she had been told. I was wrong: My aunt told me later that given the questions my mother had asked the doctor that day in his office, he had decided to be candid about the progress her disease had made and honest about her chances. He had told her that afternoon what he had told my father that morning.

And so when I spoke to my mother of pneumonia, we'd come full circle: She had lied to my father so he would have one less thing to worry about in the hospital; he—at once hopeful and disbelieving—had passed the story along to me; and my brother and I had then brought it back to her. As a family we've never been particularly good communicators, but it has never been for want of love.

My mother never had that CAT-scan, because her lungs filled so quickly with water. By the time she went to the hospital, her cough prevented her from lying flat enough for the machine to record an image of the intruder inside her.

She died in the hospital on a Sunday morning in July, moments after my father arrived. Her nurses were astonished that she had made it through the darkest part of the night, and said they thought she had hung in there for her husband. She died in his arms, a small smile in this case a surrogate for her salute.

FARMERS FLETCHER AND DON BROWN
KNEW HOW TO GROW COMMUNITY

EARLY DURING THE morning one day last month when Fletcher Brown, eighty-six, was going to be buried in Lincoln, his son-in-law, Claude Rainville, wandered past the cemetery and noticed an excavator beside his father-in-law's plot.

The hole beside the machinery was massive, and for a moment, Rainville smiled at the notion that his father-in-law, with pharaoh-like preparation, was going to bring his beloved John Deere tractor from this life into the next.

Of course, it was merely a boulder the size of a Volkswagen that was the reason the excavator was parked there that morning. Nevertheless, Fletcher had loved the time he spent on his tractor mowing the fields around town, moving great piles of earth and carting colossal tanks of sap to the family sugarhouse through snow and mud in the spring.

And though Fletcher had been too sensible to have that tractor buried with him, he had allowed himself a bit of levity when he was planning his funeral: His coffin was a John Deere shade of green and the casket was festooned with the company's iconic leaping stag on the brass plates on the corners.

Often the funerals for the very old are intimate affairs because so many friends have passed away, and there are only children and grandchildren and a smattering of acquaintances in attendance. This was not the case at Fletcher's service last month—

nor was it the case last year when Fletcher's brother, Don, died. That funeral, too, was an uncommonly crowded event.

Though the Browns had outlived many of their friends, it was a testimony to the way they had lived their lives that the church sanctuary was packed when it was time for us to bid them farewell.

A village loses something when people like Fletcher and Don pass away. We lose the tangible immediacy of their stories, such as that moment five decades ago when Robert Frost tried desperately to convince Fletcher to sell him his farm with its panoramic views of Mount Abraham. That tale, and the details of their conversation, will soon fade into myth.

We lose the knowledge of how life has changed: what farming was like before bulk tanks, what Lincoln was like before electricity. Don Brown remembered well what it felt like to bring in a wagon of hay when the wagon was pulled by a pair of field horses, and he would stand atop the bales with the animals' long reins in his hands.

Fletcher and Don were not simply good men—generous with their time and their wisdom, their personalities rich with the irony and wit that can only come from decades of winters in this New England tundra—they each understood the value of community.

Fletcher Brown loved that tractor of his, but he loved it most when he was using it in service to his neighbors: excavating the dirt around the foundation of the Old Hotel, for example, when his friends Dave and Donna Wood were renovating the inn in Lincoln last year. Don Brown savored his years owning the Lincoln General Store, but he once told me that what he enjoyed most was the opportunity the job gave him to see his neighbors daily.

When Don's son, Jim, was eulogizing his father last year, he wore his father's sports jacket because of the metaphoric significance the blazer held for him: A torch was being passed from one generation to the next.

Community is a word that has meaning because of people like Fletcher and Don. When we worry that the threads that link our communities are fraying, it is often because individuals like the Browns have passed away, and we—younger generations—have become so absorbed with ourselves that we have forgotten our friends and our neighbors.

The Browns let no one around them remain a stranger, including this urban émigré from Brooklyn, and they left no friend alone who needed help. That is a wonderful legacy to leave a town.

A FAMILY'S FAREWELL TO TIGER

IN THE WOODS beside the Gale family's sugarhouse is a small paddock, empty now for almost a month. On a particularly glorious Saturday in October—the leaves on the sugar maples glowing neon yellow in the sun, a dusting of white at the top of Mount Abraham, the sky above both a crisp and deep blue—the horse who'd called that paddock home died between a lone rock and a tree in a nearby meadow.

The earth here in Lincoln is probably filled with the bodies of old Appaloosas and Morgans, and I imagine there was somebody present at the very end to grieve for them all. In the case of Tiger—Gumbo Tiger Lily C, to be precise—there was Jennifer Gale, the horse's thirteen-year-old owner, caretaker, and friend, as well as Jennifer's parents. I think the fact Tiger had mourners is important, but it isn't unique.

What might be rare, however, is the affecting ritual that Jennifer offered her horse and her family at the end, the moving and meticulous ways she marked Tiger's passing. If a horse has to die—and, according to the veterinarian, it was indeed time for the sickly twenty-eight-year-old to be given her rest—it is good to go the way Tiger did.

There was the public farewell party Friday afternoon, one of those occasions the soul craves because the emotions are deep and complex: It's possible to juggle sorrow and joy when the horse that will die tomorrow is surrounded today by the children she's known the last years of her life.

There is young Lynn Sipsey, a seven-year-old whom Jennifer taught to ride atop Tiger. There is nine-year-old Prudence Meunier, who's been friends with Tiger since they were photographed together one day. And there, in a crowd of boys and girls between the ages of six and thirteen, is Nugget Meg, a horse-friend of Tiger's who's come by for one final visit.

Yet this isn't a dirge-filled, pre-death vigil. The children are dangling from trees, they're jumping from the loft of the Gales' barn, they're racing Tiger and Nugget Meg. They are eating absolutely massive amounts of apple cobbler.

Are they sad? No doubt; they understand what will happen tomorrow. But they are also raucous and loud and giggling sometimes, such as when Tiger tickles the palms of their hands as she munches the carrots they offer.

Jennifer's carefully choreographed celebration of Tiger's last afternoon might have made the almost preternatural quiet that filled the next morning somewhat easier for her to bear. The next day, she walked her horse the three-quarters of a mile to the meadow she'd chosen for Tiger's last home and waited there alone for her parents—Don and Jodi—and the veterinarian to arrive.

Tiger, a leopard Appaloosa, wore a pine bough wreath around her neck.

As the pair waited, three horses walked by along the road beside the pasture. Two were chestnut and one was white with black speckles. Tiger was pretty near blind at the end, so she probably didn't see them. But she heard them or smelled them or sensed them. She knew they were there. And so she whinnied a greeting of sorts in their direction, and the riders slowed their animals and waved. For a moment they watched the girl and her horse in the field, and then, perhaps sensing their presence was an intrusion, they quickly rode on.

When the veterinarian reached the meadow, he stood for a long time with a syringe the size of a thermos in his hand. If Jennifer might have preferred his hiding the needle until it was time, she kept the notion to herself; she might have suspected this was no easy task for the vet either.

Tiger went fast, her body collapsing atop her legs like the canvas seat on a director's chair once the braces have been unclasped. Jennifer stayed with her a moment, her cries considerably softer than her mother's.

But as Jodi murmured, her words rich with pain and love, "It's easy for her to be strong. She doesn't have to see her daughter's heart breaking."

BRIEF EXCURSIONS

AWAY FROM

LINCOLN

UNTETHERED IN SPAIN, SET FREE
ON ROUTE 66

WHEN I WAS TEN, my mother slept with two male strangers on an overnight train between Malaga and Madrid. She was always a very sporting woman.

My family was on one of those airline-sponsored tours in which seventy Americans visit nine cities in eleven days, and an hour is allocated to the Prado Museum and perhaps ninety minutes to the palace and grounds at El Escorial. We were going to try to see virtually the entire Iberian Peninsula in the days before and after Thanksgiving.

Fortunately, very early into this frenetic picaresque, the Caravel jet—a plane now mercifully retired in which one climbed into the passenger cabin through the bowels at the bottom rear of the aircraft—that was taking us from Malaga to Madrid was unable to land in the capital because of bad weather and had to return to Spain's south coast. Rather than stay with the tour and wait for the flight the next morning, my mother suggested that we all take the 10:00 P.M. train to Madrid, and travel, as she put it, like honest-to-God Europeans.

We did. We were in a six-person compartment with an ornate sliding wooden door that separated us from the aisle and seats that folded down into one massive six-person bed. Somehow my father, my brother, and I wound up on one half of the compartment, and my mother wound up on the other half sandwiched between two elderly gentlemen who actually wore the sorts of fedoras one expects to find in the pages of a Graham Greene novel.

They spoke a little English and my mother spoke a little Spanish, and I remember that the three of them were having a grand old time when I fell asleep. More important, my mother and father decided in the dining car over breakfast—a dining car with white linen as crisp as any I'd seen at my grandmother's, and doilies that were just as ornate—that henceforth we were going to be free of the tour, and we were going to discover Spain and Portugal on our own. We would not see as much, but what we saw we would see with some depth. And though my mother did not have the opportunity to sleep with additional men on that trip, as a family we were transported far from our original notions of what we should see and where we would go.

This is, in my mind, the essence of recreational travel: freedom. (The essence of business travel is, of course, just the opposite. Business travel is all about restrictions, logistics, and connections; about seeing how much you can wedge into a sixteen-by-twenty-four-inch carry-on, and how quickly you can conduct your business and get home.)

William Hazlitt, the nineteenth-century British essayist known today largely, alas, for sleeping with the family maid, observed, "The soul of a journey is liberty."

If Hazlitt's words have not actually become my mantra when I travel, they certainly reflect with uncanny precision both the joy I experience on the road and the method to my madness. Last year when my wife and I were in Scotland, we missed the benchmark palaces in Edinburgh and Inverness, but we managed instead to stumble across the haunting castle ruins of Dunnottar in the east and Stalker in the northwest.

Castle Stalker sits on an island no more than two acres square, perhaps a quarter mile into Loch Linnhe. It is uninhabited now, but on the shore is a railroad track that disappears straight into the water. We caught a glimpse of one of the castle's towers while traveling in our rental car behind a bus on a narrow coast road; the bus continued on, but we turned around. We asked permission of the man who lived in the house on the shore to cut through his property (the gate for his sheep was temperamental, he warned us), and followed the tracks to the pebbly beach opposite the medieval castle's remains. We picnicked there, alone on the shore with the view of the fortress to ourselves.

Dunnottar is more of an archaeological restoration project than a standing castle, but the cliff-side remains—enshrouded by the sort of soupy fog for which Scotland is justifiably famous—are well marked (including the dungeon, which was actually aboveground and offered a fine view of the North Sea if you didn't mind spending your life stooped to about half your height).

There I met a Scotswoman who loved the United States. "Someday I hope to meet someone from Seattle," she said. "I love that TV show *Frasier,* and that cute little dog they named Eddie."

The truth is that whenever my wife and I travel for pleasure, we travel with a limited itinerary at best. When we drive that great American Mother Road west, Route 66—as we have three times, because my wife is a photographer—we know that we will start in Chicago and we will arrive in Santa Monica, California, nine or ten or eleven days later, but other than that we've little idea where we will be on any given day.

Our favorite trips have always been like that: They are journeys in the best sense of the word, in which every morning is a mystery and each afternoon a surprise. One night we are in Shamrock, Texas, with its ribbon of old road and ceaselessly optimistic boosters who believe that someday the panhandle will indeed become a beckoning gateway to the Lone Star State. Another night we are in Kingman, Arizona, with its views of the stark Hualapai Mountains to the west, a range that grows salmon-colored at sunset, with a glorious yellow halo skirting the peaks.

Likewise—and this has become very important to us—no one else knows exactly where we are, either, which further deepens the sense that we are, for a change, untethered.

Grown-ups, of course, aren't supposed to feel untethered. Perhaps teenagers and college students are when they backpack across Europe with their Eurail passes. Perhaps hikers are when they take on the Appalachian Trail. But not adults who have careers, mortgages, and life insurance.

This is precisely, however, one of the greatest pleasures that travel can offer: the opportunity to experience emotions that are, figuratively as well as literally, foreign. Certainly it demands a willingness to suspend our compulsive desires for order and exactitude, and the security that comes with a guaranteed room with a guaranteed rate. And, yes, there have been times when I would have given a great deal for the security of a reservation at a Holiday Inn.

But more times than not I have savored the generous, unpredictable satisfactions that come with seat-of-the-pants travel. Suddenly the bills and the deadlines seem very far away, and there is only the altogether delectable rediscovery of what it is like to see a horizon grown boundless.

FLIRTATIOUS MINNIE PULLS UP
HER HEM

AFTER VISITING MY father this winter, my family and I went to Disney World. There I survived the most astonishing ride on the planet—the amazing "Dad's Empty Wallet," in which every credit card instantly reaches its limit—and then had the surprising experience of discovering that Minnie Mouse had a crush on me. The evidence was overwhelming.

First of all, wherever I went, Minnie was there. One day in particular stands out. My wife, my daughter, and I began the morning in the Magic Kingdom, and Minnie approached us near Goofy's roller-coaster. We had lunch at Disney's MGM Studios, and Minnie sashayed over to our table. And when we were leaving the park in the evening, she appeared out of nowhere from a faux movie set and descended upon us once more.

In between these three encounters, she seemed to be nearby all the time. We would see her constantly: on the stage by Cinderella's castle, strolling through Main Street U.S.A., signing autographs at a park entrance.

"How did Minnie get here?" my five-year-old daughter asked my wife when we saw Minnie moments apart in two separate corners.

"She's stalking your father," my wife said. When our daughter looked confused, she quickly explained, "She has a crush on Daddy."

"No, she does not!" our daughter insisted. "I've seen her kiss Mickey a thousand times, and I've never seen her kiss Daddy."

That evening when our daughter was asleep, I told my wife that it was possible we were seeing Minnie so often because there was more than one Minnie. Maybe, I hinted, it was sort of like that Santa Claus thing in the weeks before Christmas.

"Don't be naive," my wife said, her voice on the verge of deep slumber. "There's only one Minnie."

"In that case, maybe it's just our imagination," I suggested. "Maybe she's not really trailing us."

"We'll see," my wife yawned.

And the next day we did. We saw Mickey's better half everywhere. My wife counted five separate Minnie sightings and five different outfits.

"She's pulling out every dress in her closet for your father," my wife said to our daughter.

"She's pulling them out for Mickey," my daughter replied indignantly.

That night we went to dinner at a Disney World hotel where Minnie would be dining. We confirmed our suspicions: The mouse, who's supposed to have set her big, unblinking, plastic eyes on no one other than Mickey, is a vamp. She may even be a trollop. A harlot. A flirt.

At the very least, however, for one weekend she had a crush on me.

The indications? When she came to our restaurant table that night, her bloomers were showing, extending a good two inches below one of her trademark red skirts.

"Your underwear's showing," my wife said to her. (Our daughter couldn't believe that her mother would say such a thing to the mouse and offered the sort of embarrassed, anti-parent death gaze that she will use well as an adolescent.)

Did Minnie discreetly shield her bloomers? Nope. She pulled up her dress by the hem and revealed even more. "I think you're paying way too much attention to my husband," my wife told her.

Minnie tried to play coy, but she never stopped smiling. She wrapped her white-gloved paws around my chest, dipped her dinner-plate-sized ears against my retreating hairline, and gave me a very big kiss.

All the next day—our last in the Kingdom—we watched Minnie's eyes whenever we saw her, but she had made her point and her eyes never moved.

Mickey, however, had better start opening his.

MIDLIFE CRISIS RESULTS IN TAKING
PART IN THE WEENIE TRIATHLON

This column appeared nine months before New Hampshire's "Old Man of the Mountain" collapsed. I've no idea whether the triathlon's sponsors will continue to refer to this event as the "Race to the Face," or whether they will use the more precise "Race to the Place Where There Used to be a Face." I thought my young nephew might be on to something when he suggested christening it simply the "Race to the Neck."

SOMETIMES YOU SEE middle-aged men who are as sensible and wise as Ward Cleaver or Cliff Huxtable, but the truth is that most of the time you are seeing them on television. "Middle-aged man" is actually the Latin term for "Male of the species who does not vacuum and believes Mick Jagger actually looks pretty good for a guy his age."

Middle-aged men usually have at least one completely sense-less and unwise interest, and the rest of their family can only hope it is something as benign as a sudden passion for Civil War re-enactment or taking a second mortgage on the house to buy a two-seater Nissan 350Z.

My current senseless and unwise interest is the Top Notch Triathlon, a triathlon held the first Saturday in August in Franconia, New Hampshire. Nicknamed the "Race to the Face" because of the course's proximity to New Hampshire's "Old Man of the Mountain," the competition is actually a pretty weenie triathlon. It consists of a seven-mile bike ride—though every mile is uphill, and some of those miles are uphill and in the woods—a swim across the frozen slush of Echo Lake, and a two-and-a-half-mile run up the ski trails on Cannon Mountain.

My sense is that it was specifically designed for pathetic middle-aged people whose exercise consists usually of reaching under the couch for the remote, or carrying in from the car those hefty two-liter bottles of Pepsi and family-size bags of Doritos. Its slogan sums up the attitude of most participants pretty well: "The Race to the Face is tough, but it's easier than growing up."

Last year one of my wife's three sisters participated in the tri-athlon as one-third of a female team, and convinced my brother-in-law and me to start a team and join the race this year. She thought it would either be great fun to have us around her, or we'd both die of exertion and she'd stop having to share her sisters with us.

My sister-in-law, I should note, had a great time because she was on a team that came in second to last. She was the swimmer on the group, and by the time she dove into the lake the other participants were already huffing their way up Cannon Mountain, and the only people left cheering from the shore were her extended family. She had the whole lake to herself.

I'm actually not sure how her team managed to overtake one of the teams ahead of her. Maybe someone was eaten by a bear on the mountain.

In any case, what might save my brother-in-law's and my team from complete athletic ignominy next month is that my wife agreed to be the swimmer. I will bike, my brother-in-law will claw his way up the ski trails, and my wife will keep us in competition by swimming Echo Lake. She's always been a pretty good swimmer because she swims three mornings a week at the Mount Abraham High School pool, but over the last few months she's started to take her swimming more seriously.

This means that she has been buying lots of new Speedo bathing suits—which brings me back to why I have become so focused on the Top Notch Triathlon. Sure, I'm biking a little more than usual, and recently I even picked up a second pair of bike shorts for the big day. But my real interest has been in helping my wife choose her training suits. I have been a vocal and articulate proponent of the argument that the less material there is in her Speedo, the better her time will be in the water.

And because my wife knows that the only prayer our team has of not coming in last is her speed in the lake, by that first Saturday in August I should have her down to the official Speedo race thong.

Yes, we middle-aged men might have interests that are senseless and unwise . . . but at least we are predictable.

RICE PUDDING AND FRENCH EDITOR
HELP NOVICE CYCLIST SURVIVE

EIGHT DAYS AGO I survived the "Race to the Face," the first triathlon in which I was a participant.

As a brief recap for those readers who are not related to me by blood and therefore do not begin and end their Sundays with this column: I have been biking with some earnestness this year, because I was going to be one-third of a team in last week's Top Notch Triathlon in Franconia, New Hampshire. I would bike the seven miles uphill toward Franconia Notch, my wife would swim the alpine slush of Echo Lake, and my brother-in-law from Manhattan would run, walk, and—if necessary—crawl his way up to the top of Cannon Mountain.

I must confess, I didn't think a seven-mile bike ride would be all that difficult, even though it was uphill and almost half in the woods. After all, I'd been biking two and three times a week to the top of the Lincoln Gap.

Well, as a friend of mine says, "I was wrong before. I'm smarter now."

I started in the first wave of 150 cyclists (the second wave a mere two minutes behind us), and there were moments in even the first three miles in which I felt like an ailing jalopy in an interstate breakdown lane while high-performance sports cars zoomed past me. I used up so much energy trying to be competitive in the first half of the race that when I reached the portion in the woods I seriously considered pretending to be a bear and going into an early hibernation.

By the time I dismounted my bike in the transition area and handed off the wristband to my wife so she could embark upon her swim, I looked like one of the living dead from the George Romero horror movies about corpses that refuse to stay buried. Witnesses tell me that I did not exactly race with élan down to the lake to watch my wife swim, but rather staggered there in slow motion, bobbing and weaving like a drunk. My skin, I gather, was the color of craft paste.

Nevertheless I survived, and I survived in part because during the thirty-six hours before the race I had a personal trainer: My sister-in-law's French editor, José Sanchez, happened to be visiting the country and staying with my mother-in-law in New Hampshire. When he was younger, Sanchez used to ride in professional bike races, and he was a cyclist whose specialty was taking on hills.

Though he couldn't speak a whole lot of English and I couldn't speak a whole lot of French (Translation? None), through my bilingual sister-in-law he offered to discuss the number of teeth in my gears (I hadn't a clue), and which gears to use on which parts of the hills (I suggested hitching my bike to a truck and being pulled). We agreed I'd have rice pudding for breakfast, which he said was a part of many cyclists' pre-race fare.

And then on the day of the race itself, he learned two words of English to share with me as I stretched: "Work hard."

I did. Our team came in thirtieth out of sixty teams, sneaking (barely) into the top half thanks in large measure to my wife's exertion in the lake and my brother-in-law's grit on the mountain. I shaved eight minutes off my best time on my training runs, though this effort did mean that I walked like a cowboy for days and my bike looked like it had been hit by a car.

Incidentally, other Vermonters were astonishing, including triathlete Jim McIntosh, also of Lincoln. McIntosh—who actually commutes to work via bicycle over the Lincoln Gap—placed eleventh overall, and had the best time in the forty-plus age group.

Will I do this triathlon again next year? You bet. I may have been in need of a walker when I was done with my portion, but in some ways I'd never felt better: confident, healthy, and not a little proud.

And I even discovered that I liked rice pudding for breakfast.

A GARDENER CAN TAKE PRIDE IN
THOSE $17 CARROTS

LATER THIS MONTH I will be spending the night in Sugar Hill, New Hampshire, and one component of my dinner will be carrots that cost about as much as a DVD player.

I am exaggerating, but not by as much as you think.

Moreover, these are not rare and unusual carrots: The packet of seeds cost a dollar and change at the hardware store.

They are, however, a part of a backyard vegetable garden with a price tag approaching $600. Actually, "backyard vegetable garden" implies the garden is small and manageable, perhaps the length and width of a two-car garage. This garden, by comparison, is about the size of Costco.

Moreover, this three-digit figure is exclusive of all labor costs with the exception of rototilling ($50), because my sister-in-law and I were the labor, and it would be impossible to put a price tag on the joy in-laws share when they are hacking their way through lupine together underneath the hot sun, or battling armies of bugs so dense that at one point (and here I am not exaggerating) my sister-in-law thought I had put gloves on my hands.

I hadn't.

Here is what happened. Though my sister-in-law and her family live in Manhattan, they spend their summers at the ancestral homestead in northern New Hampshire. When she was a child, they used to have a vegetable garden, but they hadn't in the last thirty-five years because no one in the family would ever get to the house until July.

This year she vowed to change that. In early May she had a plot of yard tilled. I offered to plant the garden for her at the end of May, but she wanted to be a part of this joyful process, and so she and her daughter and my mother-in-law took the train to White River Junction so they could participate. The tickets totaled $372.

I agreed to meet them over Memorial Day weekend to help get the garden in.

Immediately I noticed the size of the plot: The Joad family in Steinbeck's *The Grapes of Wrath* never confronted a field this big.

"Where's the seeder?" I asked. "And the tractor?"

"The what?"

"We're planting this by hand, aren't we?"

She nodded. We began at 5:00 in the morning, possibly earlier than my sister-in-law has ever gotten up in her life. During the next two days, we planted the vegetables of her choice: tomatoes, potatoes, turnips (including something very scary-looking called kohlrabi), lettuce, zucchini, squash, watermelons (be kind—she hails from New York and is unfamiliar with New

England tundra), peppers, Swiss chard, radishes, beets, beans (lima, butter, and bush), carrots, cucumbers, and corn.

The seeds and seedlings cost $47. We spent $49 for manure and $16 for Miracle-Gro.

Since my sister-in-law was then returning to Manhattan until school ended in June, we placed bark chips and plastic mulch between the rows to minimize the meadows of weeds that were sure to pop up in her absence. The bark chips and mulch rang in at $55.

When we were done, we took comfort in the notion that if there wasn't a frost, if it rained (but not too much), if the birds didn't eat the seeds, if rabbits or deer didn't eat the early plants, if the weeds didn't become a jungle, and if the lupine didn't return en masse, there would be a mighty fine garden awaiting her return.

Exact cost: $589.

Three weeks later, I went by to see what had survived, and I was pleasantly surprised to discover that about half of the garden had made it. Nothing needed thinning, that was for sure, but the potatoes and the beets and nine of the carrots (I counted) were thriving.

In any event, if my sister-in-law were to divide $589 by the number of vegetables we will eat from that garden, it would make an organic tomato in the Antarctic look like a bargain. But then she grew these vegetables herself, and that is the reason we do this.

Self-sufficiency. Pride. The joy one can only derive from a $17 carrot.

NOTHING LIKE MOM'S BIOHAZARD
FOR DINNER

SOME YEARS AGO my wife and I were trying to spare my mother's feelings, and so we threw away a casserole dish of something she had made with seashell pasta, frozen shrimp, mock crab (not rock crab), stringy mussels, and canned clams. My mother called it *fruits del mar* or—roughly translated—*seafood so bad the smell alone will scar you for life.*

At least once she served the stuff at a dinner party. There were (Surprise!) buckets of leftovers. This was in the early 1970s, when people were downing bourbon and scotch the way today we knock back bottled water, but there wasn't enough alcohol in all of creation to make my parents' dinner guests join the clean-plate club that evening. Consequently, my brother and I ate more than our share of it the following night because—in a rare and completely uncharacteristic show of affection—we thought we should be gentle with our mother's delicate sensibilities. Our mother actually took to her grave the completely mistaken belief that we thought the casserole was not merely edible, it was scrumptious.

It wasn't. We had four dogs when I was growing up, two of which would eat their own excrement when they were bored, and none of them were willing to touch my mother's *fruits del mar.*

That's why one morning my wife and I found ourselves dumping a whole vat of the entrée—faux crab, soggy pasta shells, the dried parsley flakes from a jar—down the garbage chute at the end of the hallway in my parents' apartment building in Florida. We had arrived for a visit the night before, and so (naturally) my mother had welcomed us with her signature dish. The next morning when she saw how much remained, she chirped happily, "Oh, good, we can have leftovers tonight!"

No, we couldn't. At least I couldn't. Consequently, when my parents went out that morning to run some errands, my wife and I got rid of the remnants, telling my mother when she returned that it was just so delicious we had to eat it for breakfast. In hindsight, the casserole was probably a biohazard and the two of us violated Florida's laws regarding the proper disposal of hazardous waste.

Memories of my mother's *fruits del mar* came back to me last month because my family and I were in a restaurant, and there on the menu was the entrée. The description was a chilling parody of my mother's version: "The freshest seafood—crab or lobster or scallops—in a delicate clam sauce. Served atop our homemade pasta shells."

That night when we got home I had to call my father to tell him. "You'll never believe it," I said. "We were just out to dinner, and the restaurant actually had a gourmet version of mom's *fruits del mar.*"

"It's common here in Florida," my father said, "and it's not half-bad when it's made well." Then he laughed and added, "But your mother and I could never understand how you and your brother could eat it the way she made it. Those canned clams used to make us both gag."

I was stunned—and not a little confused. "Then why did she keep making it for us?"

"Because the two of you seemed to love it so much. We just figured it was like Velveeta—one of those foods you seemed to enjoy that struck people with normal palates as completely inedible."

Then he reminded me that during the Super Bowl this past January, it was I who had made a dish with frozen string beans, a can of toasted onion rings, and a big jar of Cheez Whiz.

"You've always had very special tastes in food," he said.

My mother and I showed our love for each other in many ways over the years before she died, but perhaps none as unpredictably O. Henry–esque as her exuberant willingness to make me the dreaded *fruits del mar* and my feigned eagerness when she served it.

AT DENVER'S GATE B42 WHEN THE WORLD WAS TRANSFORMED

I WAS AT Gate B42 at Denver International Airport when the world changed Tuesday morning. And change it did. It was not merely the southern tip of the Manhattan skyline that was tragically obliterated, it was the notion that only skyscrapers and embassies in other countries—foreign lands such as Kenya and Tanzania or cities with faraway names like Dhahran—could collapse with a literally earth-shattering suddenness.

My wife used to work in the World Trade Center when she was a bond trader and we lived in New York. She worked on the 104th floor.

Only nine months ago, my wife and I showed the two towers to our seven-year-old daughter for the first time, when we were taking her to the Statue of Liberty. We stood in the cold on the ferry and told her stories of how quickly the elevators seemed to move and what the view was like for her mother when she would gaze out the massive windows to the west and the south.

The memory stuck for our little girl, and Tuesday was a long day for her—though I wasn't there to hold her because I had been at the airport in Denver that morning.

I learned of the disaster when I called my wife to wish her good morning from the gate. It was about 7:15 A.M. my time, and 9:15 in the east.

"It's not a good morning," she said, and her voice had a quiver to it I wasn't sure I had ever heard there before. I immediately feared that something had happened at our daughter's school or to one of our parents. And then she told me what she had heard on the radio.

She explained that two planes had crashed into the towers, and at least one was a commercial jet. This was no Cessna accidentally dinging the paint on the side.

A plane crashing into one of the World Trade Center monoliths has always been one of her fears, something she sees in her mind's eye often when we fly near Manhattan and the skyline seems so close it's as if we're at eye level with the rooftops. We're not, of course, even when the plane is well into its final descent, and she had always presumed this fear was completely unfounded. No longer.

As soon as she had finished describing to me what she had heard on the radio and then seen on the television, the cell phones around me started to ring. The gate was crowded, and we all had our phones, and there was someone somewhere for virtually every one of us who wanted us to know what had happened because they loved us and were scared. They needed to hear our voices and know where we were.

Still, the magnitude of the attack wasn't yet clear, and the air-line had us board the jet for our planned flight to San Francisco a little past 7:30. I was sitting one empty seat away from a pas-senger whose brother-in-law worked in the World Trade Center, and he called on his phone everyone he could think of who might know the fate of the complex of buildings tantalizingly close to the Statue of Liberty.

All this week I have wondered why the Statue of Liberty wasn't, apparently, on the list of targets. After all, we had been shown that Washington, D.C., was not invincible, and the sym-bol of our financial and corporate wealth was devastatingly vul-nerable. Why not add to that litany the majestic icon of our freedom? Surely by mid-morning there are plenty of people on that small island, a good many of whom are likely to be children.

I will never know whether the brother-in-law of the gentleman I met on the airplane is alive. After waiting about forty-five min-utes in the plane on the ground, the pilot informed us that no more flights would be leaving until at the very least the end of the day, and in a voice that was even and calm he told us why. He told us that the number of planes that had crashed now totaled three, and that a fourth one seemed to be missing. We were to disembark.

I exited the plane and sat stunned in the very seat at the gate where my wife had informed me that the world had been forever transformed. I called her again, and the one piece of good news she had was that a friend of ours who we presumed had been at the World Trade Center that morning had been fired at the end of last month. My wife had tracked her down at her home while I'd been on the edge of the tarmac.

Even this kernel of relief dried up quickly, however, when I saw the man from the plane whose brother-in-law had been at work at the tip of the island. He passed by me, squeezing his cell phone against his ear, and his skin was paler than it had seemed when we had spoken together on the inside of the plane. I told myself it was just the lighting in the terminal versus the lighting in the cabin, but I didn't really believe this was the case.

I wasn't sure what I should do. I was at the very beginning of a lengthy book tour, and I was supposed to be heading west, but I no longer had any desire to talk about my novel. Likewise, I couldn't believe there was a soul on the planet who would have any interest, either.

I wanted only to go home, but even that was impossible. An airport representative informed us that the airport was going to close. We were to take the underground trains from our concourse back to the main terminal, and from there we were to vacate the airport. It wasn't going to reopen for at least twenty-four hours.

I was lucky: The hotel where I had been staying hadn't even changed the sheets on the bed on which I'd slept, and my publisher was able to get me the very same room. Other travelers weren't so fortunate.

Still, that afternoon when I took a long walk I felt farther from home than I ever had in my life, and the sky above—though the fathomless blue that I crave in the fall—made me lonely. I knew, by then, that there wasn't a commercial jet in the sky. They'd all landed as quickly as they could.

Imagine, I thought. Other than those F-16s on patrol, a sky without planes.

For all of us there are moments that represent horrific turning points in our lives and images that we will never be able to forget: the paisley-shaped plumes of smoke that trailed the space shuttle *Challenger* through the atmosphere after it exploded; the rubble that surrounded the skeletal remains of the Murrah Federal Building in Oklahoma City; and, of course, the footage we revisited the past few days of Pearl Harbor and the assassination of John Kennedy.

I doubt any of those images, however, will scar the soul of a nation as deeply as what we all watched on television or in person this week: a plane slicing into one of the World Trade Center towers, its twin beside it already ablaze; two 110-story buildings collapsing in upon themselves in mere seconds in storms of smoke and soot and debris. A rolling wave of ash that tumbled like lava down the streets of the financial district.

My sense is that this nation will recover. We will not be bullied, and we will not be frightened; we will give meaning to the lives of the people who died by going on—by refusing to see our way of life annihilated.

But we will all know where we were when the comfort and security we take for granted was destroyed as surely as the skyline of lower Manhattan. And that moment, for me, will be a gate at an airport far from home.

TALKING THEN, TALKING NOW

IN THE DAYS immediately after terrorists transformed four commercial passenger jets into guided missiles last year and forever altered our world, people talked. We talked of our immediate past and where we had been September 11.

Two weeks later I agreed to stumble through the vestiges of a largely canceled book tour in Boston, and I must have had fifteen conversations about the attacks that late September day with people I was meeting for the first time. Everyone needed to share where they were, what they had experienced, and their personal interpretation of how things had changed.

All the conversations that day seemed to share one thing: the desire to portray oneself as having a connection, however tenuous or vague, to the victims of the attack. One woman told me that she had gone that weekend to a memorial service for a friend of a friend. Another person said that she'd flown twice on the same Boston-based flight that would auger into the World Trade Center's north tower. A man shared with me his fears for his nephew who was living in Brooklyn Heights and who was at the moment enduring the fumes from the fires in lower Manhattan.

There were more, and I certainly wasn't shy with my own anecdotes: the fact that I had been at Denver International Airport when the attacks occurred and was stranded in Denver for a week, or the footnote that my wife once worked on the 104th floor of one of the World Trade Center towers.

Throughout the day in Boston I was with a woman who was conspicuously quiet: my media escort, the individual my publisher had retained to take me to the area bookstores and radio stations.

Around lunchtime I wondered why she was so silent when people shared their tales of 9/11. My sense was that suddenly we were a nation of talkers—except for this woman. And so I asked her where she had been on the morning of 9/11.

She rolled her eyes and told me—not a trace of self-pity in her voice—that she had begun the day watching as her brother perished because he worked on an upper floor of one of the towers, and then she helped novelist Jane Hamilton find a way back to her home in the Midwest.

After a moment she added: "If I entered the conversations you've been having today, I would have stopped them dead in their tracks. There's a lot of one-upmanship going on right now, and I just don't feel like playing."

Ever since then, I've been leery of talking about where I was on 9/11, or what I was experiencing. It's not that I no longer believe it's healthy or helpful to reflect on my specific place in the cosmos on 9/11. But my grief is different from that experienced by the families of the nearly three thousand people who died, the people who still live in lower Manhattan, or the people who rose to the daunting task of cleaning up the mess: carting away a literal mountain of rubble, trying to identify the tens of thousands of body parts, or even replacing the windows that were shattered at the nearby apartment buildings.

My grief—the grief of most Americans—is for the loss of that feeling of invulnerability we've savored since the Cold War ended. In that regard it's very real. Likewise, our sorrow for what the victims endured before they died and for their families who are left mourning is with us every single day.

Nevertheless, when we talk this week of the anniversary, let us not simply recall where we were a year ago. Let us not merely sit before the mind-numbing parade of images—the towers, the Pentagon, the living, the dead, the missing who will never be found—that are monopolizing our TV screens and being used to sell a small library of new books.

Let us honor the victims instead by discussing as well energy policies that do not demand foreign oil, and behavior that is less dependent upon fossil fuel. Let us talk of peace in the Middle

East. Let us celebrate our incomprehensible bounties while imagining how we can share that largesse with the rest of the world. And, yes, let us envision ways to spread democracy—ways that do not involve the carnage that comes with all war.

In short, let us talk this week not only of where we were, but also of where we can be.

CANDY HEARTS WOULD HAVE BEWILDERED ARMENIAN GRANDPARENTS

MY ARMENIAN GRANDPARENTS did not invest much energy in Valentine's Day. They took it about as seriously as they took Arbor Day.

Nevertheless, I view their marriage as one of the great love stories to which I am attached by blood. I know it wasn't perfect: Leo and Higoohi Bohjalian had a relationship as complex as any, and their happiness together was leavened by their share of disappointment, discontent, and deeply personal dissatisfactions. But it was also a liaison that traveled successfully from Istanbul to Paris to a suburb of New York City, and a marriage that lasted half a century.

Moreover, it was a marriage that succeeded despite the fact it had been arranged by their families before they met, a relationship brokered by a seemingly endless array of aunts and uncles and cousins and friends, while my grandfather was living in the United States and my grandmother was living in Turkey.

My grandfather had immigrated to America at the beginning of the twentieth century, after spending his adolescence as—consider this an exercise in creative résumé writing—an "importer-exporter": He was a hashish courier between Egypt and Europe. In Manhattan he went from washing windows to repairing watches for an upscale Wall Street firm that specialized in clock restoration. No one in my family is quite sure how this career change was managed.

He was either very good with those watches or he'd saved a lot of money from his days as a courier, because he built a three-story brick house twenty minutes from Manhattan that I know from old photographs was every bit as large in reality as it is in memory.

And then he needed a wife, which was where my grandmother came in. My grandmother's father had been killed in the murky, violent miasma that swallowed a million Armenians in 1915, but she and her mother were spared. And her mother—my great-grandmother—was willing to broker her lovely daughter to Leo since this successful man planned to bring her to that fantasyland of freedom and opportunity and (more important) safety.

Everyone convened in Paris in 1927 for a summit, and the deal was sealed—and, soon after that, consummated. It was touch and go whether my married grandparents would get my grandmother through Ellis Island in early 1928 in time for my father to be born on American soil.

When I was a child, I occasionally stayed with my grandparents when my parents were away, and so I glimpsed how the two of them lived.

The day would begin with my grandmother preparing for my grandfather his usual breakfast: a fried lamb chop and American cereal. My grandfather loved American cereal, and he used to mix

CHRIS BOHJALIAN

Rice Krispies and Corn Flakes in a dish the size of a punch bowl. Then he went to his office in Manhattan, and I would explore the house in which my father was raised. Occasionally, my grandmother would try (and fail) to interest me in dense books of Armenian hieroglyphics.

In the evening when my grandfather returned, he would play the oud—a sort of Middle Eastern lute—and then my grand-parents would talk . . . forever. Sometimes they spoke English, but often it was Turkish or Armenian. They would talk for what seemed an eternity before dinner, they would talk during dinner, and they would still be talking when I went to bed. Sometimes they would adjourn to the basement where my grandparents had an ornate pool table, and there my grandmother would quickly dispatch my grandfather. Though she never learned to drive, she could have made a very good living hustling pool.

When my grandfather wasn't at work, my grandparents were inseparable, their own small world of two. They needed no one, and my sense is they thought the notion of a day to celebrate romance with chocolate candy and paper hearts was somewhere between harebrained and inane.

Even so, their marriage ended only when my grandfather, then a very old man, passed away one night in his sleep, after a day spent playing his beloved oud for his beloved wife.

ON MOTHER'S DAY, GRANDMOTHER
BRIEFLY RETURNED

THE WORDS—two syllables, really—should have been spoken by a toddler: "Who dat?"

My grandmother was just shy of eighty at the time, and as she asked her husband, my grandfather, this question, she was pointing at me with a hand so gnarled by arthritis that she was actually aiming her knuckles at me, rather than the tip of her finger.

"That's Christopher," my grandfather said.

"Not Warren?" she asked, turning away from me for the first time since my mother and I had arrived in their front hall in Florida.

"No," he answered calmly, "it's not Warren."

Warren was her son—my uncle. I was twenty-two then, and so my Uncle Warren had to have been in his mid-fifties. He was tall and blond and had jumped from an airplane into France as a member of the 101st Airborne in the Second World War. He had a movie star's chiseled jaw. A person would have had to work hard to confuse us.

"Who's Christopher?" she continued, and my grandfather patiently explained to her that she had a daughter named Annalee and I was one of Annalee's boys. Annalee, at that moment, was surveying the kitchen, discovering that my grandfather had installed child-guard locks on the cabinets because he was fearful that his wife would confuse Drano with Cool Whip or Windex with tea.

This was the last time I would see my grandmother, a Mother's Day weekend visit my own mother and I made together to Florida not quite two decades ago.

My grandmother's descent into Alzheimer's had not been as swift as we had feared, but it had been steady. It had taken close to five years for a suddenly cantankerous obsession with temperature (always it was either too hot or too cold) and a benign forgetfulness to evolve into full-blown dementia. Still, my grandfather was determined to keep her at home, a testimony both to the impressive depths of his love for her and his faith that he could provide her better care than a stranger. One of my mother's reasons for our visit was to convince my grandfather that in fact he could not: My grandmother needed the ministrations of a nursing home.

Nevertheless, my mother was also hopeful that her own mother would be sufficiently lucid for one last Mother's Day brunch at a restaurant on the ocean, or to enjoy one last walk along the beaches of Longboat Key in search of shells. These were pretty unrealistic desires. My grandmother was no longer even tying her own shoes or cutting her own meat. Consequently, I was expecting a fairly somber long weekend. And, in truth, most of those three days were either poignant reminders of my grandparents' love—such as when my grandfather gently would wash my grandmother's hair in the sink because she could no longer do it herself—or unpleasantly grim indications of their situation. Twice that weekend I was awakened by my grandmother shouting that there was a burglar in their house (me), while during the day she continued to presume I was Warren.

Still, my grandmother had one last surprise.

She was an organist, and for years had played show tunes and Christmas carols at the Macy's department store in White Plains, New York. Between her arthritis and her Alzheimer's, however, she rarely touched her own organ at that point in her life. On Mother's Day morning, the day my mother and I were going to return to New York, she surprised us both by playing—badly, but recognizably—the wondrously saccharine, mawkishly sentimental ballad "Believe Me, If All Those Endearing Young Charms."

It was among my mother's favorite songs, even butchered as it was by my grandmother. She told her mother how much she loved it.

"I remember," my grandmother said, and then she sighed.

She would die soon after that. I am not sure she ever had the slightest idea who I was that weekend. But for one moment on Mother's Day, she recognized her own daughter, and even on their final day together she remembered what made that woman, once a girl, smile.

THE LADIES' ROOM JUST INSIDE
TOMORROWLAND: A SHORT STORY

This is the only short story in this book, the only piece of writing that is fiction by design—rather than fiction because my memory has become a spaghetti colander. I have included it because although it is wholly invented, it does express the panic I certainly experienced (and the anxiety that I believe any sentient parent must feel) the first time my young daughter ventured alone into a bathroom in a public place.

HE LEANED AGAINST the cement wall, a father who was no longer young with a daughter who was, and listened briefly to the sounds of the toilets flushing.

He checked his watch, noting the speed with which the second hand was traveling around the small clock's face—the black line was moving in tiny fits and starts, and he wondered if it had always moved like that and he had simply never noticed, or whether the battery was about to go—and memorized the exact time.

It was 5:17. Five-seventeen in the afternoon.

His daughter had entered alone into the ladies' room at exactly 5:17—5:17 and seven seconds, if he was going to be precise (and he was)—in the afternoon, the sky just starting to darken as the sun fell somewhere far to the west of Frontierland.

It was January and the days were short, and he realized that if they stayed for the fireworks at 7:00 P.M. (and, it was inevitable, they would), he would have to hold on tight to his daughter's hand as they tumbled into the roiling stream of people leaving the park at one time for their cars. He'd never witnessed the exodus firsthand, but he'd heard, he'd heard: Virtually the entire human contents of Disney World converging on Main Street at once—a horde tens of thousands strong being funneled together toward the turnstiles and the trams and that ridiculous, retro metro monorail.

It was like a fight for the lifeboats, he'd been told, in which a man's most noble instincts would be subsumed completely by the urge to flee . . . and live.

Yes, he decided, he would insist that his daughter hold his

hand. Or allow herself to be carried. Or accept the fact that he was going to tie her to his back like a thirty-eight-pound, three-and-a-half-foot-tall papoose. But he would not lose her.

She had just turned six, and—though she still believed that Snow White was precisely who she said she was, and Cinderella really did live in that phantasmagorically garish castle that served as the Magic Kingdom's centerpiece—these days she was feigning the walk, the distance, and the incredulity that marked an adolescent.

She was an only child, the youngest girl in her first-grade class, as well as the smallest. And though there were other girls and boys who lived with only a mother or a father, she was the only one who lived with a single parent because half the equation had died.

The two of them had been in the park since 10:15 A.M., and this was the first time that the girl had expressed any interest in going to the bathroom. After a lengthy discussion before leaving Boston the night before, they had agreed that she would be allowed to enter the ladies' room alone when she had to pee, and he would wait outside. He had wanted her to use the men's rooms so he could keep her—or, at least, her ankles beneath a stall door—in plain sight, but she had fought hard against this indignity.

And, in truth, he wasn't sure that he wanted her in the men's room with him anyway. How in the world do you explain a urinal to a six-year-old girl? Why in hell would you want to?

But this was their first trip alone, just the two of them, the first time, in fact, that they had ventured together beyond Massachusetts—beyond their street in Newton, practically—since the girl's mother had died in October. They were still figuring things out, and bathrooms were a part of the puzzle.

"And what'll I do when you have to go to the bathroom?" she

had asked, once they had agreed that she would be allowed to venture alone into ladies' rooms. "I don't want to wait around inside the men's room!"

He didn't want that, either. The truth was they had never been one of those peace-love-and-tie-dye families in which parents and children bathed together or swam naked together or— God forbid—went to the bathroom with anything like visual or aural proximity. She hadn't seen him naked since she was seven or eight months old and he would take her into the bath with him when he'd come home from work, and bounce her around in the shallow water in the tub. He hadn't seen her naked since she'd been in preschool—and, he imagined, she would be appalled if she understood that as recently as two years ago she hadn't cared if he walked into the bathroom to hand her a towel before she started the long climb over the porcelain side of the tub.

"I won't go to the bathroom until we return to our motel, I promise," he'd said, convinced that this was the only workable solution. After all, what was he going to do, hand her off to some stranger while he disappeared inside the men's room? Leave her standing alone in the open air in the midst of Disney World's crowds and chaos and rides? Not a prayer. He'd sooner cause permanent kidney damage than lose his little girl because he'd had a second cup of coffee at breakfast.

He glanced at his watch. Five-eighteen.

She'd been alone in the ladies' room for just under a minute. Perhaps half a dozen women—old and young, some with gray hair, one with a stud in her nose and lines of steel balls along the cartilage of both ears—had come and gone through the arching entrance in the time that he'd stood there.

He wished he'd been able to find a handicapped bathroom like the one they'd discovered at the airport. It was as big as a studio apartment, but housed a single stall, which meant he could be there with his daughter while giving her the privacy she demanded.

He wondered suddenly if he looked like a pervert. Here he was, a slightly plump forty-one-year-old in khaki shorts, standing outside one of the ladies' rooms in Tomorrowland. A balding guy whose thinning straw-colored hair was largely hidden by an aging Red Sox cap. He realized he was wearing sunglasses and quickly removed them. He didn't need them at this time of day, unless he had something to hide.

Which, of course, he did not.

He tried to ignore the sensation—sensation? who was he kidding, this was pressure—in his bladder and groin that he had begun to feel perhaps an hour earlier, when they had ridden Splash Mountain. All that water. The rivulets that ran down the cavernous walls as their little boat bounced along the inside of the man-made Ozark Mountain. The fact that the ride had made his seat—and then, therefore, his pants—wet. But he could last another two hours. Or, if there was a logjam at the exit, three.

Still, the sounds of the toilets and the faucets inside the ladies' room, a small orchestra of rushing water barely fifteen yards away, didn't help. But there was nothing to be done. He wished a mother with a little girl—one child, just one, so it wouldn't be too much of an inconvenience—would approach the bathroom so he could ask her if his daughter was OK. Someone like his own wife, perhaps. But there didn't seem to be a doppelgänger present right then.

A thought crossed his mind, and the vague unease he'd been feeling about allowing his daughter to leave his sight abruptly became more pronounced: Somewhere in this world were bathrooms with two entrances. It was inevitable. And, perhaps, he had inadvertently stumbled upon one. He had escorted his little girl, that single person on the planet he cherished above all others, to a bathroom that was a free ticket to separation or abduction or (it was possible) something far worse.

He felt his skin growing clammy, because he understood that one of two things was about to happen: Either his daughter was going to emerge from that second entrance, wherever it was, and become lost forever in the massive amusement park as she searched for her father. Or a child molester or serial killer was waiting just outside that other entrance for a child exactly like his, because child molesters had known all along what he had just discovered: this rare, dual-entranced bathroom. It was a playground for perverts. A rec room for psychos.

Either way, unless he went into the ladies' room that very second and rescued his daughter, she would be gone from him forever. Unless he took a deep breath that moment and ventured inside the concrete-and-stucco inner sanctum, he would never see his little girl again. This reality was obvious.

He shook his head and reminded himself there was no reason to believe there was a second entrance. He was being ridiculous. It was barely 5:19. His daughter had been inside the bathroom a mere two minutes. Any second now, she would shuffle out in her sandals and shorts, pushing her hair behind her ears exactly the way her teenage baby-sitters did back home. The two of them would find a place in the park for dinner and then settle in for the fireworks.

His daughter was fine. Yes, indeed.

Unless there was a window. Maybe that was how she would be taken from him. Through a window. He realized that he had seen lots of women exiting the bathroom, but he wasn't sure he had seen any go in who hadn't already come out, meaning his daughter might be alone in there with no one to protect her from—how could he have missed it?—that kidnapper with the rolling bucket and mop. That kidnapper who had been pretending to be a park employee all day, just waiting for the moment when he'd be alone in the bathroom with a small child. In an instant he'd have her gagged and they'd be gone, the two of them disappearing forever into the January twilight.

He saw an older woman with bluish hair and a Camp Mickey sweatshirt approaching the bathroom, her mouth working hard on what had to be an apple-fritter-sized piece of chewing gum. She wasn't a young mom with a child in tow, but she would do, and he was about to ask her to check on his little girl, make sure she was all right—good God, simply make sure she was even still inside the damn bathroom!—but before he could make his own mouth open, she was through the archway and gone.

But that was good, too. It meant that the criminally insane, incompetent-to-stand-trial sociopath who had spent his day in the bathroom just waiting for a small child on which to prey could no longer operate with impunity. There was a third person inside there. Did it matter that his daughter's protector was a gum-chewing senior citizen in a Camp Mickey sweatshirt? Certainly not.

Unless this woman happened to be dangerous. He knew from an article he had read a year ago that there were forty-three women on death row, and some of them were senior citizens. Child murderers.

And, clearly, the woman with the bluish hair was strong enough to steal or murder his child, if that was something she wanted to do.

But why would anyone want to do that, ever? Why would anyone want to hurt a child? Yet bad things happened all the time, and they happened to kids every bit as adorable as his. Look at what she was already having to endure: Her mother had died.

He could make no mistake about this: A bad thing—a very bad thing—could happen at any moment, and there was no way he could even begin to explain or justify or rationalize the grotesque bits of tragedy that appeared in this world out of nowhere. A physical exam with something unexpected in the blood work. That was all it had taken to begin the slide—and *slide* was precisely the right word, he decided, with its connotations of a quick and slippery and out-of-control descent—that had done in his wife. Five months, start to finish. Five months.

Every single day, children disappeared in a positively incalculable fraction of that amount of time. A blink. They disappeared on their way home from school, they disappeared as they played on their front lawns, they disappeared from grocery stores while the parents pressed their thumbs into melons in the extra-wide aisles of fruit.

And, he had to assume, they disappeared from Disney World. The only reason you never heard about those kids or saw them on milk cartons or the TV news was because the Disney empire controlled the world. Didn't they own some TV network? Of course they did. They probably owned all 500 channels on the satellite dish that sat outside the guest-bedroom window back home.

It was 5:19 and 55 seconds. Almost 5:20. She'd been in there three minutes.

Her bladder couldn't possibly hold three minutes of pee. His could—he figured it had about three hours' in there right now—but not hers. Something clearly had happened, and that's when it hit him: No one was interested in abducting her from the bathroom, because that wasn't possible. There was no second entrance;

there weren't even any windows. Instead, someone had hurt her and left her bleeding or unconscious in a far corner stall. It had been one of the last women he'd seen leave the bathroom. The tall woman who'd been wearing the scarf and the sunglasses.

He knew firsthand there was no need for sunglasses at this time of day, unless your intentions were suspect. (Hadn't he taken his off?) That woman had done something: She had done something awful.

He resolved firmly that if his daughter wasn't outside in sixty seconds, he would go in after her. Four minutes was his limit; it was all he could endure.

But what if four minutes was too long and he lost her—lost her forever? Then what? He couldn't imagine. He just couldn't imagine. He tried to slow his breathing while wiping his forehead under his cap with his handkerchief. He was sweating, sweating profusely—a human fountain oozing fluids from every pore—even though it was the end of the day and he was in the shade. The cotton square in his hand was now the color of oatmeal from his perspiration, and it was as damp as a used beach towel.

Inside, he heard another great whoosh of water, and a moment later the woman in the Camp Mickey sweatshirt strolled through the arch, applying a coat of burgundy-colored lipstick across her mouth as she walked. She had eyeglasses the size of coffee cup saucers, and he decided to ask her if she had seen a little girl in the bathroom, a charming first-grader in a gray denim baseball cap with what looked like a fish on the front but was in actuality a whale—a souvenir from their summer trip to Cape Cod, their last as a family of three.

He lunged toward the woman, one hand before him, and stumbled, recovering awkwardly.

"Harold!" she cried, moving quickly away from him, her eyes

wide behind the goggles that passed for eyeglasses. An older man appeared out of nowhere, wide-shouldered and robust, with a mound of hair on his head the color of ash from a woodstove. He took the woman by the elbow and led her away, where they disappeared quickly into the crowds that milled by the souvenir stands and ice cream carts, and the conga lines that snaked around almost every ride.

He wondered if they were going to report him to security, and he was about to meet the Disney World Secret Police. But he didn't care about that, all he wanted was to see his daughter—all he wanted was to see that little person with eyes as green as her mother's, scuffing her sandal-clad feet through the ladies' room arch.

He turned, oblivious to his resolution to wait a full four minutes, uncaring that he still had a solid fifteen seconds to go, and started into the ladies' room—was he crying out her name as he walked? He hoped not, but he thought he might be, when he realized he could see the line of white sinks opposite the stalls, and she was standing on her toes, whipping the last drops of water from her small fingers.

In his head he murmured thank you, thank you, and it was all he could do not to fall on his knees or, perhaps, spread wide his arms in a giant "V." Victory. Hallelujah. Amen. He turned, hoping to retreat before she knew he was there, but it was too late. She'd seen him.

When she emerged, her arms were folded across her chest and she was shaking her head. He knew she was about to chastise him for checking on her, for worrying, but she saw his tears and she paused. She looked up at him, then straight at him because he was kneeling before her, and, understanding everything, she touched her palm to his cheek. He lifted her and stood, and held her against him for a long time, trying to make light of his panic but not really caring that his jokes must have sounded pathetic and lame.

He promised her that he would try not to worry next time, though he was quite sure that he would. He felt her nodding before she buried her head in the small pillow of flesh where his shoulder met his neck, her chin a pear against his collarbone, and her body relaxed completely in his arms.

Acknowledgments

I WROTE MY first story for the *Burlington Free Press* in February 1988 (four years before I would start writing my weekly column for the newspaper). It was a six-hundred-word article about advertising in Vermont, and it was the first time my name had appeared professionally in print in any capacity other than as a novelist or short story writer. My editor then was Candace Page, an immensely gifted journalist. I will always be grateful to her for her willingness to toss her years of wisdom and experience aside, and give me twenty-one column inches to call home.

I've had a great many editors over the last decade and a half who were as patient as they were talented, as insightful as they were inspiring. Among the very best? At the *Free Press* I've had the privilege of writing for Joe Cutts, Geoff Gevalt, Mickey Hirten, Rebecca Holt, Stephen Kiernan, Stephen Mease, Casey Seiler, Ron Thornburg, Mike Townsend, and Julie Warwick. At the *Boston Globe,* I will always be appreciative that I had the opportunity to work with—and learn from—Bennie DiNardo, Louise Kennedy, Nick King, and Julie Michaels.

Finally, I am deeply indebted to Jennifer Carroll, currently director of news development at the Gannett Company. When Jennifer was the executive editor for the *Burlington Free Press* in the mid-1990s, we talked often about "Idyll Banter," and it was she who encouraged me constantly to write about Lincoln. She saw before I did that this one small town was a microcosm for a changing America, and there were a series of stories here just waiting to be written.

About the Author

CHRIS BOHJALIAN is the author of eight novels, including *Midwives* (a *Publishers Weekly* Best Book), *The Buffalo Soldier,* and *Trans-Sister Radio.* In 2002, he won the New England Book Award. His work has been translated into seventeen languages and published in twenty countries. He lives in Vermont with his wife and daughter. Visit him at www.chrisbohjalian.com.